THE Teacher's Survival GUIDE

by Jenny Gray

Norte del Rio High School, Sacramento, California

Consultant: *James R. Erickson*, Principal,

Norte del Rio High School, Sacramento, California

Drawings by *Robert Haydock*

FEARON PUBLISHERS **Palo Alto, Calif.**

preface

Experienced teachers may find this book a waste of time. It wasn't written for them. It is directed to the young men and women who have at length learned the educator's "open sesame" and are now ready for the splendid adventures that await them in the pedagogical cave. Many of these new teachers are so lacking in experience they are hard put to tell a j.d. from a genie, much less know how to transform themselves into the latter for the purpose of dealing with the former when the occasion demands. Without guidance, the new teacher may find himself backed into a corner by his rambunctious students. Not long after that, he will yield to overwhelming temptation and abandon his chosen career —a loss both to him and to the community so critically in need of his services.

It is easy to forget that our public schools are, above all, public. The con men, prostitutes, schizophrenics, manic-depressives, rapists, thieves, and murderers who will make up our prison and mental hospital populations twenty-five years from now are sitting in our public school classrooms as you read these words. They must be dealt with—hopefully in such a skillful manner that there will be fewer con men, prostitutes, schizophrenics, manic-depressives, rapists, thieves, and murderers—but dealt with, none the less.

My purpose in *The Teacher's Survival Guide* is to help the novice over the discipline rough spots so that his classroom time can be devoted to teaching rather than policing.

Sacramento, California
August, 1966

JENNY GRAY

iii

contents

one

The Problem

Control in the classroom is necessary for several reasons, all of them good. First of all, a school is for learning; a teacher, by definition, is committed to this goal. The teacher is there to teach the students. Where rowdiness and insolence hold sway, learning still takes place, certainly; but the results aren't likely to be compatible with the curriculum goals of the school, no matter how permissive the school's philosophy.

Secondly, from the moment he signs a contract, the teacher shares with the public school a tacit obligation to society. In the main, we allow ourselves to be governed by duly elected persons and their representatives. This is the only way our society can function in an orderly way. It is not good, therefore, that our young people become adept at the fine art of insurrection. The teacher who allows students to victimize him in his classroom indirectly encourages them to victimize the man at the newsstand, the stranger in the park, and the cop on his beat.

1

True, there are emotionally unstable students who, for therapeutic reasons, need to express their hostilities in some way. In these cases, it is even more important for the teacher to enlist the aid of other professionals on the school staff so that a student's aggression may be rechanneled into wholesome outlets. Above all, the teacher should avoid encouraging further development along unwholesome lines.

The hostile student is a victim of his own anger. He cannot save himself—he cannot hope to make himself acceptable to society—without the help of the professional people around him. If they fail to show him good ways to substitute for his bad ways and help him to make the transition, where can he turn? Furthermore, the teacher has an obligation to the students who are the actual or potential victims of the emotional cripple. He must maintain control of his class both to restrain the one and to protect the other.

Their protestations to the contrary notwithstanding, the need of young people for control, guidance, and protection from their own folly is as real as their need for food and sleep. Teacher popularity polls beyond number indicate that students reserve their highest accolades for the teacher who, ignoring good-natured taunts and complaints, maintains the steady pressure required to get the best behavior and the best work from them. New teachers invariably react with surprise when they discover for the first time that the vast majority of young people prefer firmly-controlled, well-planned classes. An existentialist, pot-party atmosphere is fun for a while, but it soon palls for all but the farthest-out young patrons.

This only proves, of course, that adolescents are people like the rest of us. Human beings hunger for and respond favorably to order. We all want to know what's going to happen and when. We want to know what the rules are and what will happen if they are disobeyed. We want to know where we stand.

Good discipline is necessary for maintaining good teacher relations, good public relations, and a proper school image.

The immediate result of a poorly controlled classroom is overstimulated students. A class with an ineffectual teacher is as much fun as a fifty-man donnybrook in the parking lot. At the end of the class period, the bell rings and Teacher A's class rushes like a banzai charge to the classroom of Teacher B. Teacher B must then devote ten or fifteen minutes to Operation Quell before the students are in the proper frame of mind to work. Teacher B is seldom amused by this.

Geographical neighbors are upset as well as chronological neighbors. The noise from a rowdy class can hinder learning activities in adjacent rooms or, if the walls are thin, in an entire wing or even the whole school. Visitors notice the pandemonium. Eyebrows are raised and word passes through the community, from whence it ultimately returns to perch, like a bird of doom, in the office of the school administrator. The teacher who allows such disturbance to continue un-checked is not likely to endear himself to his colleagues, and even less to the principal in the direct line of fire from the school's patrons.

One of the best reasons for maintaining an orderly class-room is that the teacher has an obligation to himself. If he can't control his students, he'll be out of a job before long. There's less likelihood he'll be asked to resign (although he probably will be, in time) than there is that he'll resign of his own volition because his physical and emotional health are beginning to crack under the strain. Depending on the state of his nerves, it will take perhaps a week, perhaps a year, for his students to drive him out. But drive him out they will. Day after day, week after week, the pattern will be the same:

"Hey! Somebody broke the pencil sharpener."

"Bob did. I saw him. He took off the handle. Search him, Teacher."

"You're a—XO**@—liar. I did not."

"Bob, stop swearing and give me the handle to that pencil sharpener!"

"I ain't got it. You all the time accusing me of stuff I didn't do!"

"Who threw that book?"

"What book? I didn't see no book."

"I can't sharpen my pencil."

"How's anybody gonna do anything when we can't sharpen our pencils? Helluva class *this* is!"

"Did you take the handle off the pencil sharpener?"

"*No!* So help me God, I ain't got it! Go ahead, search me!"

"Will you *stop swearing!*"

"How'm I gonna sharpen my pencil?"

"*Owwww!* Herb hit me! @*//·X you, you *** *** ** *
*****!" (Pow!)

"*Sit down! Cut that out!*"

"He hit me! You gonna let him get by with that?"

"We *are not* going to have that kind of language in this
room!"

"What language you talkin' about? Whad I say wrong?"

Doubling up on tranquilizers takes care of the shakes after-
ward but doesn't diminish the horror as it's occurring. Nor
does it diminish the teacher's sickening realization that from
some source he must summon the strength to overcome this
situation by himself. Nobody can help him. It's the loneliest
feeling in the world. Scant wonder that some settle for the
less heady environment of a real estate office.

The punishment visited upon a teacher by an insulting,
belligerent class is so great, both directly and indirectly, that
it is surprising he allows such a situation to arise at all. Or
allows it to arise more than once, let's say. Yet, there are a
number of teacher-candidates who, by virtue of temperament and background, are predestined for discipline trouble
before they ever face a class.

Paradoxically, the teacher with a natural affection for
young people and deep faith in their inherent goodness will
be in for trouble. The first time a student turns in disgust
from a reprimand muttering, "Aw, cool it," this teacher
will be loath to fix the offender with an icy stare and curtly
ask him to repeat what he said. He is more likely to think
that if he ignores such incidents they will go away. They
won't. They will get worse.

Some individuals are too kind, too sympathetic, too peace-loving ever to make very effective teachers. They can't say no and make it stick. No matter how plentiful the evidence may be to the contrary, they resist the realization that for the first weeks, or perhaps the first months, those creatures on the other side of his desk are The Enemy and must be dealt with accordingly.

School people euphemistically say students "put new teachers to the test." In most schools, this "test" has all the flavor of a Peking third degree. From the students' point of view, it makes a gruesome kind of sense. They want to find out how much this new teacher will tolerate, not only re-garding actual physical misbehavior in the classroom, but about cheating, handing in homework assignments, "borrow-ing" books from the room, and the rest of it.

However logical the students' motives may be, for the teacher himself it amounts to a nasty initiation period. "Love is not love which alters when it alteration finds." And alas, for some teachers, it wasn't really love at all. Upon finding that young people can, indeed, be rude and malicious on occasion, they no longer care for them as much as they thought they did. They retire from the field, and this is doubtless best for everyone concerned.

Other teachers love them anyway, alteration or not, and after a few uncomfortable weeks learn to contend with them the way they are, faults and all. Such a teacher has qualities that will one day make him a master teacher, if he is not prematurely overwhelmed by what he will feel to be his failure.

It does not follow (horrors!) that if you dislike adolescents you will have no problems and therefore will be a good teacher. Teen-agers sense hostility in the adults around them and, given the most meager opportunity for retaliation, are quick to take advantage of it. The ugliest surprises of all are reserved for this teacher.

Still others who will be in for trouble are those who have spent their own tender years in the sheltering confines of gentle, soft-spoken families. The unrestrained speech of to-day's teen-agers sets their teeth on edge. When exposed for the first time to the brutal candor of the young ("This room stinks. Can I open a window?"), they feel unduly offended and their reaction is out of all proportion to what is de-manded by the occasion. Confidences of the uninhibited shock them and they say so. The furtively-scrawled grafitti on the blackboard revolts them and they say so.

In common with the ministry, our profession attracts any number of candidates seeking a genteel position. From a distance, a career in education does appear to be genteel. In actuality, it is far from genteel. The public school educator comes in contact with everything from petty theft to incest —with the traumatic results of human depravity that defy belief.

The mass media may cling to its stereotype of the un-sullied, wide-eyed schoolmarm, and what the public doesn't know won't hurt it. But what the prospective teacher doesn't know or refuses to face *can* hurt him. If he has a squeamish stomach, he should find a career elsewhere.

A teacher-candidate who is too timid to ask is in for un-pleasantness. He may not be sure which problems of student control he is responsible for and which should be handled by the vice-principal, the nurse, or the counselor. Perhaps a student in his class spends the whole period, every day, crying. Another may insist he has a spastic colon; he asks to be excused to go to the restroom every day and is gone most of the period. Not being sure what to do, and reluctant to attract attention to his own uncertainty, the teacher procrastinates and thus aggravates situations that demand prompt attention.

Such a quandary is likely to develop for a person who has had little prior contact with young people similar to his student population. He can't distinguish between slightly abnormal behavior, which he is expected to handle himself, and extremely abnormal behavior, which should be referred to others on the school staff. This can happen not only to new teachers, but also to a teacher who moves from a senior to a junior high school, or from a "ghetto" school to a "country club" school. What is normal in one place may be abnormal in the other. All of these people must expect to undergo a period of adjustment.

Occasionally a teacher is foredoomed to have control problems because of what might be called "educational miscasting." A natural-born kindergarten teacher may inadvertently prepare for teaching at the junior high level, where she soon has discipline problems beyond her capacity to handle. A

scholarly, introspective teacher who would find quick success with the sons and daughters of college professors in a
university community may find himself in the gut-level
environment of an inner-city school where his tastes make
him a funny guy indeed. Hapless fifth graders may be
taught close-order drill by a martinet who would be happier
expending his energy tangling with adolescents than divert-
ing younger children from their marbles and hopscotch.

The commonest misplacements are not due to teachers'
unfortunate decisions but to school district expediency.
Good teachers nowadays are hard to find. A candidate who
has prepared to teach history may be assigned a load of
math or English classes because that year the district has
more history teachers than it needs and can't find math or
English teachers. So, in addition to his other orientation difficulties, the teacher must provide instruction in a subject he
feels unsure of—or, perhaps, actively dislikes. His lack of
preparation is soon evident to the students and becomes a
source of control trouble.

All of these people have been miscast. They are teaching
in the wrong places—wrong for them and wrong for their
students. The bitter outcome of such a situation is that, as
the years pass, the teacher's antipathy towards his students
grows. Perhaps he has family obligations to meet and is un-
able to make the necessary financial sacrifice to start over
somewhere else. He finds himself trapped and tends more
and more to vent his discontent on his students, a tragic
predicament.

The plight of the history teacher with the math classes
may be buried for years, especially in a large school, unless
the teacher takes it upon himself to press his case for a new
assignment with the principal. To get the grease, the wheel
needn't necessarily squeak loudly enough to be menacing—
just persistently enough to be slightly annoying. But squeak
he probably must to get the assignment he wants.

Anyone entering teaching should think seriously about where he can contribute his best teaching efforts. He should attempt as many "dry runs" as possible. Maybe he will find students more attractive singly or at a distance than face to face in a group. If so, he need not teach them at all! The field of education is no longer the narrow vocation it once was. A quarter-century ago, one was a classroom teacher or a principal, or perhaps both if the school were small. Over the years, schools have added the services of business managers, librarians, psychometrists, speech therapists, attendance officers, television personnel, and film technicians, to name a few. It takes all kinds to make the world of education go 'round, these days.

two

Stop Trouble Before It Starts

"No one can tell you how to control your classes; this is something you must find out for yourself." Sound familiar?

Don't believe a word of it. You learn to control a class the same way you learn to weave, serve a buffet dinner for twelve, or talk to New York taxi drivers. You read the directions, study the diagram, and talk to people who have done it. Then you do it yourself.

First of all, you need to have your goal clearly in mind. Otherwise, how will you know if you achieved it?

Your goal, stated in all its ludicrous candor, is to make your students obey you. That's what this book is about. Whether we adults like it or not, discovering imaginative new ways to challenge authority is the great parlor game of American youth. As a teacher, you must checkmate all such attempts so that your students, discouraged by repeated failure, give up on you and shift their attention to other targets.

You don't especially want students to obey you with fear, because then they won't tell you important things like "The superintendent is coming down the hall to visit your room." It's better if they obey you in somewhat the same spirit they would obey the captain of a team—because you're a good Joe and you're better than they are at whatever it is you're doing. This is called "respect." Although it might rankle to be forced to keep on earning it week in, week out, year in, year out, that's the price you pay for tenure.

The acid test, which you must expect to fail the first semester, is what happens when you're absent from the room. The students may behave well when you're with them, but what do they do when you're called to the phone? Or what do they do with a substitute?

If you are successful at building good discipline habits in your students, they should be depended upon to regulate themselves in your absence—to finish the assignment, to leave the room in as good order as they found it. The ultimately successful teacher, like the ultimately successful parent, makes the child independent of him. The teacher strives to develop in the student those qualities of self-discipline which will one day enable him to teach himself.

You want to see an increase in good sportsmanship. There should be more consideration for the other fellow (including you!), a greater willingness to share and take turns. There should be a greater tendency in the group to be friendly and extend support, not to a few, but to all its members, to visitors, and to newly-enrolled students. There should be a "we-ship" in your classes, born of the security that roots and flourishes when students realize that no individual will be threatened unless he himself originates the threat.

When it comes to noise, the decible count is only one measure of good control. You want your classes to be quiet, yes; but a quiet class doesn't necessarily mean there is good control. The members may all be asleep. Ask yourself the

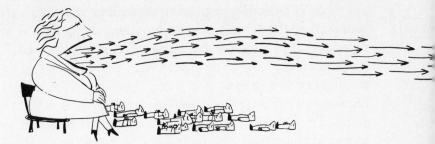

same question your supervisor will ask when he enters your room to observe: Is there learning going on here? Are the students quiet because they are absorbed in their school work, or are they merely cowed?

There are noisy classes and noisy classes. A successful— a truly successful—skit, debate, or discussion will generate an uproar of sorts. But this is "good" noise. This is learning noise, one of the nicest sounds in the world to hear. When fifteen or twenty adolescents are sitting on the edges of their seats, emitting squeals and grunts of suppressed excitement, waving hands frantically for permission to recite, you are doing a fine job of teaching.

There is the comfortable buzzing sound when small groups in the room are working together or students have paired off to study. There is that throbbing, electric silence when every student is so absorbed in what he is reading that he has completely lost touch with you, the school, the noises outside in the street—everything. Across the room a student finishes. He looks up dazed, closes his book, and stretches. You go to his desk, finger on your lips, to remind him not to disturb the others.

"Boy, that was a good story!" he whispers.

Marvelous, marvelous.

The best learning is not merely something the student does with his mind, but something he experiences as a total human being. It must engulf him so completely he forgets himself, forgets disappointments, anxieties, and resentments.

The noise in a classroom lets you know if this is happening. For a teacher, these learning noises are the payoff. Once you earn your place as captain of the team, you have the power to produce the learning noise you desire in your classroom.

How Do You Look?

Funny, isn't it, how success in achieving any goal always seems to depend on the little things? Good classroom control depends on little things, sometimes even superficial things— like the way you look.

Nobody ever pretended that schoolteachers have a monopoly on comeliness. In fact, particularly in young teachers, beauty of face and form can be a handicap when the student population is age twelve or over. Discipline problems for women teachers tend to rise in direct ratio to the height of the heel and the hem of the skirt. The same factor works against the handsome young male teacher who can't understand why girls in his classes are so recalcitrant. Roiling glands make for noisy kids.

But grooming is something else. Anybody can be well-groomed. And if he's working with teen-agers, he'd jolly well better be! Although teacher rating forms used by administrators commonly devote space to judgment on this point, the score given by the most fastidious principal will never be as severe as the judgment on the rating sheets the students carry around in their heads.

Adolescents outdo every other segment of the population in finding fault. Discussion of the faults of others—including teachers, of course, because they're handy—forms a dreary staple of teen-age conversation. If you don't believe it, eavesdrop. You'll learn a lot. For instance, you'll learn a teacher can forget his deodorant one day and find himself on the students' black list for a week. Bad breath, body odors, untidy hair, dirty hands, and soiled clothing are less easily forgiven than a poor grasp of the subject matter; and they make control much more difficult.

How Do You Sound?

To control a class, you must be heard at the back of the room. You must be heard *clearly* at the back of the room. If you command the required volume and clear diction and possess, in addition, a speaking voice so flexible in range and timbre that it can direct briskly, coax with sweet reasonableness, or encourage gently enough to melt stones, you are lucky beyond anyone's right to expect.

If you do not possess such a voice, it is well worth several dollars' tuition and several semesters' work in some speech department to develop it. While there, you might make certain you aren't burdened with other speech handicaps, such as lisping, stuttering, and whistling sibilants. Be sure you aren't saying "he don't" for "he doesn't"; and if you're from south of the Mason-Dixon Line, make sure you aren't saying "that's rat" for "that's right."

How Is Your P.Q. (Planning Quotient)?

Another big little thing the teacher needs for good control is the self-discipline necessary to get organized and stay organized. Once children advance beyond the primary grades, they're hard to fool. Gaps of time while the teacher hunts this, goes to get that, gives the wrong directions and then must correct them, or fiddles with the equipment, are the hallmark of the amateur and play hob with the image of competence the teacher is trying to maintain. It's the pro who knows what he will need, has it, and keeps things moving.

When students are busily engrossed in schoolwork that has meaning for them and understand how they are to go about it, they simply do not misbehave. If there is good teaching, there will probably be good control, too. Each supports the other.

The Environment

Make your classroom attractive. Pots of plastic philo-dendron require neither water nor a sunny spot and go far towards brightening up the place. Colorful pictures taped to construction paper relieve drabness. Bulletin boards can be superb visual aids for teaching a unit, setting a mood, or getting across a point. However, if he hasn't already learned it in an audio-visual class, the new teacher should be warned that a good bulletin board display is the result of hours of planning and work. Over the years, most teachers build excellent files of display materials and ideas; but the novice, short of both the time to prepare such materials and the money to buy them ready-made, is likely to have a lean time of it in the bulletin board department at first.

Anticipate Your Physical Limitations

Take some thought for your nerves. When pressures build too high, your patience evaporates and discipline problems rush in to fill the vacuum. The best way to avoid pressure on your first assignment is to drop by school at least a week early to get your textbooks, teacher's manuals, curriculum guides, lesson plan book, etc., so you can get your homework out of the way ahead of time.

There will be interludes in your teaching career when you will stay one day ahead of the students; but this kind of high-wire stunt requires considerable skill and *sang-froid*, both of which you will develop later but don't have now. Once school starts, records, memos, directives, bulletins, and what-have-you will fly past your head so fast you'll barely have time to dodge, let alone see where they hit. Do yourself a favor and study your textbooks. Get everything put together in your mind while you still have a mind left.

When you outline your lesson plans for the first few weeks, pay attention to the energy factor. Some lesson plans take a lot out of you; some don't. Avoid, for example, scheduling a lesson plan that calls for showing two short films (to be projected by you) plus a chalkboard-illustrated lecture (given by you), the whole thing to be repeated for five or six successive classes. By 1 P.M. you won't care if school keeps or not, and by 4 P.M. there won't be enough left of you to warrant the attention of a self-respecting taxidermist. This is assuming you have only one preparation. If you have two or more, it's even more important to avoid squandering your physical resources, because there'll be even greater demands on your mental ones.

Practice. It isn't enough to load, run, and rewind the tape, film, or filmstrip once. Go over this operation often enough so you can talk and give your attention to the students while you're doing it.

Your lesson plans are more likely to be too short than too long. For every class, always have something extra to send the students on to in case they finish early. When caught with your lesson plans down—and you will be (the film won't arrive, or the ditto machine will break down and you can't run off the test you planned to give) allow the students the extra time for study. *Do not* turn them loose for a "free time" session that, for the new teacher especially, is likely to get out of hand.

Let Students Know What To Expect

Decide what formula you are going to follow in computing your grades. Will tests count for half of the semester grade or a third? Will reports or themes be required? If so, when? How will they average in on the semester grade? What arrangements will you have for the student to make up work he misses when he is absent?

Learn to write out instructions for homework assignments so that they are clear and easy for even your slowest students to understand. Then set aside a conspicuous place in your classroom, perhaps a section of the chalkboard, where homework assignments will always be written for easy student reference. Deadlines for projects, reports, and the like, should appear here. Never let a student drag out the old "but I didn't know what I was supposed to do" chestnut. Keep this little assignment board up to date and he must either produce the assignment or admit his own, not your, negligence.

How's Your Frown?

Spend some time practicing a menacing, evil glare in front of your bathroom mirror. Pack all the threatening disapproval you can muster into a nasty, wide-eyed, stare. (A flicking jaw muscle adds a certain dash.) To govern by eye control is a talent of the master teacher. It saves voice and feet. Learn how to do it.

Know Who's Coming

You will have class rosters before classes begin. Take the time to study them. Getting to know your students as quickly as possible is an essential for good control. It will take you two or three days, perhaps a week, to get your seating charts in order.

When the students first come into your classroom, you can expect the compulsive talkers to arrange themselves so as to get the most conversational mileage out of the least distance. You will have to reseat them. The potential drop-outs, in an effort to get as far away from school as the law allows, will choose the back seats. They are the ones you will want to seat closest to your desk, for they will need the most help—not recrimination, help.

Starting off on the Right Foot

At the beginning of every period, you will call your class to order. The first day or two you won't need to. The students will be on their good behavior, both for your benefit and for the benefit of many of their fellow students, who will also be new to them. They will be quiet because they are curious. As the newness wears off, the chatter level will rise. When the room is noisy, wait. Don't begin until the students have noticed you standing before them and have stopped talking. You may need to help matters along. "May I have your attention, please?" "May I have *your* attention, too, Joe?" "I'm waiting for you, Evelyn." Don't shout. If you do, you'll lose.

Do something that first day to show your subject matter proficiency. Read a selection from a play, make a tool, draw a picture, or kick a ball. Tell your students something about yourself. Married? Children? Where did you go to college? Former experiences in jobs, teaching, armed forces? Win trophies in wrestling? Karate? Knife-throwing? Little things like that.

From the first day, refuse to let students get up and walk out on you in mid-sentence when the bell rings to signal the end of the period. The teacher dismisses the class, not the bell.

Several Don't's

Don't let students call you by your first name. Kids this cheeky will need to have the message clearly spelled out for them in words of one syllable. "Don't call me Pete. I am your teacher. Call me Mr. Smith."

Don't tolerate naps. "Sleep on your own time, not mine. Sorry."

Don't tolerate throwing in the classroom. This will start innocently enough with a student tossing a pencil to his buddy in the next row, or a wad of paper into the waste-paper basket six feet away. "Go get the paper. Return to your seat. Get up. *Carry* it to the wastebasket. Drop it in. Return to your seat. Don't throw *anything, any time*, in this room."

Don't tolerate profanity. "The place for locker room language is in the locker room, not here." Glare when you say it.

Don't tolerate even playful scuffling. "Any more horsing around like that and you're in serious trouble. Sit down and keep your hands and feet to yourself." *Really* glare when you say this.

Your Desk Is Yours

From the beginning, refuse to let students get in the habit of making themselves at home around your desk. Don't let them sit in your chair when you're not in it or hang over you when you are. Girls, especially, will give men teachers the business about this. If not outmaneuvered, they will lean in provocative ways. The male teacher may find it necessary to pull out a drawer to force a girl student to stand back, put a stack of books on the edge of the desk where she's leaning, or best of all, stand up. Train your students to raise their hands when they need help. When they do, go to them. Stay on your feet.

Go Slow at First

In the classroom, there is a happy medium to be sought between friendliness and aloofness. If you have spent a great deal of time with young people before, you won't need to seek this happy medium at all; you will automatically assume the attitude that's right for you.

Then, too, especially if you're in a school or with classes you know ahead of time will be tough, you'll move that attitude a bit to the "aloof" side of the scale those first few days of school. The tougher the school, the farther to that side of the scale you'll move.

Seasoned teachers always "start out hard." They don't smile much. They don't crack jokes. Why? A teacher can't find out how a class is going to shape up until he's been with the group for a week or two. With some classes, you find within a few days you can relax a bit, perhaps a lot. But with other classes, you must exercise vigilance every minute the students are in the room; you won't be able to smile at them until you tell them good-by in June. It isn't always individual students that make the difference, either. Sometimes it's the "mix" that's particularly volatile.

Coach; Don't Criticize

The way you take hold the first few days of school will determine how your students size you up and react to you; so will your attitude towards them. Teaching is, after all, a matter of changing behavior. The way you feel about your students will show in the thousand-and-one ways you go about effecting these changes. A student's theme may come back to him with "Your paragraphs are too long" written across the top. This is criticism—negative, cold, and not particularly effective. The teacher may have written instead, "Your written work will be more readable if you try shorter paragraphs." This is coaching, which gets better results. Does this kind of thing make a difference in classroom control? You better believe it!

The Formula

Play it cool. It's the 007 image that's "in." Eric von Stroheim is "out." You can lose face by yelling. There's even an 007 formula you can use to deal with misbehavior in the classroom. It goes like this:

1. A student is shooting rubber bands at his girl friend across the aisle. Look directly at him while continuing your lecture. Do not pause. Never allow a discipline

problem to interrupt your work if you can possibly help it.

2. Usually, you will be able to catch the erring student's eye. Deliver the baleful glare you practiced in front of the mirror. If the student continues his disruptive behavior, point your finger at him and shake your head to indicate clearly to him that he is to stop. Continue your lecture without pause.

3. If he is so engrossed in his misbehavior that he doesn't realize you have seen him, continue your lecture and walk slowly towards his seat. As your voice grows louder, he will become conscious of your approach and glance in your direction.

4. By this time, he has gotten the message all right. If he persists, you are dealing with a student who is deliberately challenging you. Do not lose your temper. Do not for one moment lose the train of thought of the classroom work. Continue to move towards him.

5. If he stops before you arrive at his seat, continue on your way to him, anyway. Stand beside him and conduct your class from there for a minute or so. Let him sweat. When the other students' attention is elsewhere, lean over the offending student and, in a whisper or voice so low that no one else can hear, tell him emphatically that when you correct him you expect him to obey immediately. Do not argue.

6. If you know he has seen you but persists in his misbehavior even after you have arrived at his seat, lean over him and whisper or speak very low in his ear. No one but the culprit should hear what you say. Deliver the nastiest, most abusive attack on his character, his personality, and his appearance that you are capable of. Do not threaten. You don't need to; you are in charge in your classroom and you intend to stay in charge. Do not use profanity. Do not malign members of his

family or allude to his race, creed, or ethnic background. *Do not touch him.* Nothing should register on your face but a pleasant, rather noncommital expression. The weapon is what you are saying to him. Any entertainment that is provided for the class is in the squirming of Mr. Funnybones himself. Ignore any attempt at rebuttal on his part. Continue to insult him with the pleasant expression on your face. He knows instinctively that if he loses his temper, his strategy backfires. It was you he intended to make a laughingstock, not himself. Only later will he realize that he dare not repeat to his friends what you said to him. After all, some of the things you said might be things his friends already think but don't say to his face. When he has subsided, tell him you don't want any more trouble out of him.

7. Then, forget it. Continue with your class as though nothing had happened. In your future dealings with that student, act as though nothing has happened. Of the seven points, this last one is the most important for good long-term classroom control. You will have differences with many students over the school year. To store up these incidents like old photographs in an album is to deny the student the freedom to redeem himself and grow into a better person. Take care of the offense *when it happens.* Take care of it *thoroughly.* And then forget it.

Sometimes you will be irritated to discover that although you are willing to forget a classroom incident, the student isn't. Although you caught him red-handed tearing the page out of the classroom dictionary and he richly deserved the stiff reprimand you gave him, he may withdraw into a black sulk for several days. Ignore it. He is punishing you for punishing him! It will require the patience of Job to keep from popping him a good one on the mouth, but don't. Someday his wife will. He can't sue *her*.

One cautionary note before we leave the classroom set-to. You won't always catch the culprit red-handed. Unless you are such a marvel of human engineering that you can referee twelve ping-pong games at once, eight of which are being played behind a four-foot hedge, a time will inevitably come when you chew out a student for something he really didn't do. It isn't because of his denial that you will know this. All students but the most docile will deny having thrown the eraser across the room or tripping someone as he walked up the aisle. What may arouse your suspicion that you tapped the wrong offender will be the intense degree of his surprise and indignation. He will stammer and redden; veins will stand out in his neck. Let matters stand for the moment. As the class is leaving, invent a pretext to call aside a student who was sitting next to or behind the accused and see what you can find out privately. If you were wrong, quietly go to his seat the next day and apologize. He'll spread the word, never fear. You will gain far more by admitting you were wrong than you would by clinging to your error.

Contraband

From time to time you will have to confiscate things. Although most students, when asked, will wait until after class to show their friends the bauble made in shop class or the snake's skull picked up on the way to school, there will be some who either can't or won't wait; and the resulting hubbub creates a disturbance. In that case, you must sometimes ask that the attention-getter be given to you for safekeeping until class is over. Never keep such an item. It is not yours. It is a prized possession and should be returned to the owner at the end of the period.

Corporal Punishment

In the teacher's handbook that you'll receive when you start to work, there will be a section on corporal punishment. The teacher should know the state laws and the district policy regarding corporal punishment as well as he knows his name. Regardless of whether state law does or does not expressly forbid it, a new teacher is well advised *never* to touch a student in anger. *Never*. This means shoving, shaking, pinching, jerking at clothing, stepping on toes, and so on. In cases of incorrigible students (and there are such things; the man who said there were no bad boys was seeing through a glass eye darkly), the school has recourse to suspension or expulsion. Later, when you have time, you will want to familiarize yourself with these laws, too.

"The Office"

There may or may not be anything in the teacher's handbook about sending students to the vice-principal's office. When you start to work, nobody ever comes right out and tells you just how this arrangement works. Your principal wants you to feel the security of knowing that the administration will back you up when discipline problems arise. Yet if every teacher sent students to "the office" for every minor infraction, a larger staff would be required in the office than in the classrooms! So the matter is glossed over in the expectation that if the teacher runs into something he can't handle, he'll send the student down. And this is exactly what you should do, with no apologies, no defensive explanations whatever, so long as you send the student *as a last resort.*

There are degrees of punishment for student offenses. The rank order goes something like this:

1st offense: "Joe, please be quiet."

2nd offense: "Joe, did you hear me? I asked you to be quiet."

3rd offense: (privately) "When I tell you to be quiet, that's just what I want you to do. Open your book and get to work."

4th offense: (also privately) "Listen to me, you pimply little bag of greasy hot air, etc., etc."

5th offense: (outside in the hall). "I told you four times to stop talking and you're still talking. So what's with you?"

6th offense: Send to the office.

You will find that a crisis with a student will often build up over a period of several days. Thus, you are able to warn the vice-principal about the student before you find it necessary to send him down, which for the new teacher is by far the best policy. The vice-principal will already know not only what the misbehavior is but what steps you have taken to straighten it out.

By and large, a school operates better if everybody concerned understands that the office is a final recourse. If you consistently avoid sending students down for trivial offenses, you can depend on the office to jump on your culprit with great vigor when the proper time comes. If you send down five students a day, they'll get a slap on the wrist and that's about all. If you send down one a week, he'll get a royal chewing-out. If you send one a month, he'll get some

kind of gosh-awful punishment detail, or even a paddling if
the law allows. If you send down only one student a year,
you might never see the kid again. The vice-principal will
think the offense was so bad that maybe the kid should be
kicked out!

The office is like a savings account. Draw on it all the time
and there's not much protection. Save up for when you really
need it.

Handbook Rules

In the teacher's handbook will be several pages devoted to
do's and don't's about gum, tardies, and class deportment.
Read them carefully. A typed or printed summary of these
rules posted on the bulletin board is a good idea. Twenty
minutes of class time the first day of school devoted to discussing them with your students is an even better idea.
Many students will know the rules quite well already. What
none of them will know is whether or not *you* know them
and, if so, how strictly you intend to enforce them.

There is always student pressure to interpret these rules
liberally or, better still, ignore them, and administrative
pressure to interpret them strictly. The teacher's judgment
must be mature enough to steer a wise course between the
two. The new teacher, short on experience and long on the
desire to make good, is best advised to hew as closely to the
book as possible. When in doubt, ask.

Security

Many schools have strict policies about money in teachers' desks. Proceeds from the candy sale, club dues, and so
on, should be turned in promptly. Instance after instance
can be cited where a school was broken into during the
night (repair windows and door locks, $12) and a locked desk

hacked to bits (replace desk, $150). Net gain to the thief: $2.50 in the P.T.A. membership dues envelope.

Every school has its own standard procedures for securing the classroom before leaving at night. This information will be in the teacher's handbook. In some districts the custodians lock windows and doors; in others the teachers customarily do this. In schools with untrustworthy neighbors and low budgets, all audio-visual equipment must be locked up at night, in others it may remain in place in the room, set up and ready for use from day to day.

Schools with a high break-in rate may prohibit teachers from locking desks, cabinets, and files. Classroom doors may be left unlocked and standing open at night. So are vending machines. Locks are more expensive to replace and repair than the pencils and candy bars the thieves might steal. All student records, supplies, money and audio-visual equipment is locked in the vault at night. Teachers are warned not to leave valuable personal effects in their rooms.

It's poor policy for a teacher ever to carry more than a dollar or two of his own money while at school. Make change for students? If a youngster needs change for more than a dollar bill, he should be sent to the office for it. A student with a bill bigger than a one is suspect, anyway.

If the teacher intends to go shopping after school and has cashed a check for this purpose, he might put the bills in an envelope and give it to the office personnel for safekeeping. A woman teacher should never leave her handbag where students will be tempted to rifle it. Expensive jewelry is a silly risk. It's in poor taste, too.

Keep up Your Gradebook

The seeds of poor control are often sown in sloppy records. Did the student fail to turn in his written report on time because he was absent? He insists he was, but your gradebook does not show this absence. Are you keeping a girl from graduating because you gave her bad grades, or has she kept herself from graduating because she made the bad grade with no help from you at all? Your gradebook should reflect these things, and it should reflect them accurately and consistently.

More than classroom control, there's a legal matter at stake in attendance records. In every school across the land, there is some kind of formal nose count every morning to furnish the raw data from which the school's Average Daily Attendance is computed. This is the same formidable ADA about which school battles are fought in state legislatures and by means of which many millions of dollars are allocated to local school districts from state treasuries. ADA, because it controls the state's flow of money to the school, is a fiscal matter; as such, it is subject to periodic audit by state officials. Incorrect nose counts cause embarrassment. *Your* incorrect nose count can cause *you* embarrassment.

It's better policy to "compute" grades than to "give" them. If the student is convinced his grade depends on his effort to learn the subject matter, he will learn the subject matter. If his grade depends on learning how to butter up the teacher so the teacher will "give" him things, he will learn to butter up the teacher.

Don't allow yourself to be intimidated by parents or, sometimes, surprisingly enough, other teachers who insist that "Keith is a straight-A student" when your gradebook clearly shows Keith to be a B-minus student in your class. Don't argue. Just bring out your gradebook.

Hidden Dangers of Pet-ism

Students respect a teacher who doesn't have pets, who enforces rules with equal vigor for all students. You wouldn't be human if you didn't have favorites, of course. What needs

to be guarded against is the temptation to favor them openly —"openly" to other students or "openly" to *them*.

The same will hold true for a class. What often happens is that the favored student or the favored class will get out of line (partly your fault; you will relax more with the students or with the class you enjoy) and you will have some straightening-out to do. As a result of one thing and another, you can count on it that the class you find delightful the first week of school *won't* be the one you are finding delightful by the first of November. There will be a different favorite by Christmas and still another one by Easter. But this should remain your private business; nothing but harm will result if you let the students know it.

Be Consistent

Consistency may be the hobgoblin of little minds, but its opposite is the bugaboo of good classroom management. When you change something, you call attention to it.

When you teach, the thing you want to call attention to is not the seating arrangement or the heading on students' papers, but the material you are teaching. Therefore, bring variety into lectures, demonstrations, and class discussions.

But it works against your interests as a teacher and compounds your control problems to interpret school rules strictly today and ignore them tomorrow, check roll one way today and another way tomorrow, or use a different method every day for collecting students' papers. Decide at the beginning how you want these things done, and stick to your procedure.

Personal relationships with students are subject to the same rules as personal relationships with members of your family, friends, or anybody else. When you blow hot and cold, nobody knows what to expect and your presence generates a certain uneasiness. This is even more true of the students who are subject to your authority in the classroom.

Tact is necessary. The teacher must be frank in order to achieve his goal, but the truth need not go stark naked. "Put clothes on the truth" by telling a story, or by using such phrases as "Had you ever thought that perhaps if you did so-and-so that . . .?"

Don't Be Bulldozed

Teen-agers get carried away with their enthusiasms. They will demand your permission to let them do such-and-such *now*, even though neither they nor you know anything about the business at hand. When you are hurried into a yes or no decision, always say no. Then take time to get the facts. It is easier to change the no to yes later than the yes to no.

Whose Fault?

"Mama made me the punk I am today" is a favorite theme of the young, and no wonder. In today's pseudo-Freudian culture, they hear variations on this theme in every medium from comic books to musical comedy. In many cases, the teacher will have an opportunity to meet the student's mother and, having done so, will be inclined to agree with the student. But the teacher's *raison d'être* is to bring about change for the better, not to accept imperfection passively.

If the teacher goes along with the sterile philosophy that "it's all Mama's fault," he will soon find himself with nothing to chew on but his own saliva.

Granting that imperfection is Mama's fault, what then? Mama is clearly imperfect, too. Who is to blame for *her* imperfection, Grandma? And is Great-grandma to blame for Grandma's imperfection? And Great-great-grandma to blame, and so on and on? Today's generation of punks isn't a unique phenomenon of the twentieth century; there have been generations of punks ever since Cain.

Well, then, what is today's generation of punks going to do about it? Will they continue to visit the sins of punkism on their own children and on their children's children, or do they intend to break the vicious chain and do something constructive to stop being a punk? It is in their power to do so. It is in the teacher's power to make them want to do so.

Hellooooo Down There!

The new teacher needs to know when to speak up and when to shut up. In a large school, a new teacher is likely to disappear like a rock in a bucket of mud. His difficulties may go undiscovered for months, even years. Don't let this happen to you. You're too young to die. Let people know you're there. Establish communication lines with the counselors, the dean of boys, and the vice-principal and drop by various offices from time to time to talk over discipline problems that bother you. The janitors, the secretaries, the nurse, and the cafeteria people can give you all kinds of useful information. Cultivate friendship with experienced teachers who can answer your questions.

Spend some time in the teacher's lounge or the faculty dining room *listening*. At this stage of your development, you have more to gain by listening to experienced teachers talk than by hovering over your desk in your room grading papers. Take the papers home and hover over them on your own time. Your first year will be a hundred per cent hell anyway so you may as well resign yourself to an eighteen-hour day and relax.

Knowing when to shut up is as important as knowing when to speak up. For example, never discuss a student with or within earshot of another student. This kind of thing invariably finds its way back to the one you least want to hear it, well-steeped in vitriol. Don't go around bearing tales to students or anybody else about fellow staff members, their troubles or shortcomings. A fink by any other name (*i.e.*, "unprofessional person") still smells bad.

Keep Your Perspective

We school people deal in book learning only, and there are many other kinds—some that go so far beyond us that we are left behind in a cloud of dust. Remind yourself that Albert Einstein failed his entrance examinations to college, that Herbert Hoover repeated freshman English at Stanford and failed it the second time as well as the first, and that Dwight Eisenhower ranked next to the bottom in his West Point graduating class. You will be obliged to fail many students, because that's the way everybody plays the game. But when you must fail a student, you can refuse to let the mark become a personal rejection.

Allow yourself ten full-dress blunders your first year. That should hit it about right. As you fall in and out of your successive pits of error, note that the earth has not been riven asunder and the skies have not turned blood red. Nothing like that happened when the country's other two million teachers made their first-year mistakes. No disaster is ever so dreadful that it can't be remedied by time and a sense of humor.

The best thing you can hope for your first year—and I fervently wish it for you—is that you have both students and colleagues with whom you can share a good laugh.

three

Getting Down to Cases

The teacher must wait years to see the harvest of his labors. Sometimes it isn't until the children of his former students come to him that he finds he may pride himself on his efforts of twenty years before. By expending great effort, he was then able to teach the first generation to "talk English good." Thanks to that effort, the second generation may learn to "speak English well."

This is true in the area of curriculum. It is also true in the area of common ethics. The school must take the long view. There is the boy who is caught with a cache of pencils stolen from the school commissary. The parents are summoned to the school for a conference. Upon being told of the theft, the distraught mother, who works as a stenographer in a government office, upbraids her son for taking such a foolish risk. It wasn't necessary, she tells him; only the week before she had copped a dozen new pencils from her office to replenish the supply at home!

The mother has been stealing for fifteen years. No one has ever caught her or made her feel it was wrong in any

35

way. She sees no reason why she shouldn't go on stealing
property that doesn't belong to her for another fifteen years,
and she probably will.

For the boy, it is different. He steals from the school once,
is caught, and will remember the unpleasant consequences
for a long time to come. Who knows, with a little luck, perhaps the third generation won't steal at all!

Keeping petty crime nipped in the bud is as much the
obligation of the teacher as giving a subject-matter test. The
difficulty with the new teacher is that, due to his innocence,
he's apt to nip in all the wrong places. The person on the
school staff most likely to show him the right places will be
the administrator who heads up the discipline department.
His title may be vice-principal, dean of boys, or head
counselor. This hapless gentleman is full-time chastiser,
chaser-downer, and (when all else fails) chucker-outer of
evildoers. He maintains liaison with the police department,
parole officers, the juvenile court, detention home officials,
and parents of young offenders—sometimes even the parole
officers of the parents! He is the official who plays the Stern
Father Figure for the school establishment. He does the
dirty work. He seldom deals with the majority of decent
kids who people our secondary schools, only with the small
minority consisting of thugs, punks, and brats.

The daily pressures on the SFF are fantastic. Indignant
daddies and mommies will threaten to come to school and
tear him apart if he lays a hand on Sonny, and he frequently
does and sometimes they do. The tires on his car are more
apt to be slashed than anyone else's. His life will be threatened fairly regularly. He will have an unlisted telephone so
he can get some peace at home. He may also have a facial tic
and an ulcer or two.

This man won't be playing the SFF because he enjoys it.
He'll be doing it because somebody must do it, and do it
well, if the school isn't to fall into the hands of its lawless
elements. Moreover, this assignment happens to be one of

the rungs in the ladder that leads to the principal's job. Every principal has gone through it at one time or another. When he did well as SFF, he was promoted to Benign Father Figure, in which position he snarls less and exercises total authority in matters that are the true concern of the school, teaching and learning.

By all means, the new teacher should get to know the SFF and give him all the support he can. Nobody will appreciate it more, and nobody is in a better position to return favors.

Now it's time to discuss specific classroom situations that demand action on the part of the teacher. They range from minor occurrences encountered daily (gum chewing), to problems that may take place in his classroom less frequently, perhaps only once every five years (serious theft).

Classroom Buzz

As prevalent as the common cold and twice as hard to combat is a phenomenon best known as "classroom buzz." A group of compulsive adolescent chatterers can buzz a teacher right out of business.

Classroom buzz is made up of one part necessary student conversation ("May I borrow your study guide for a minute?") and four parts unnecessary student conversation ("Who was that creep with Ruth in the hall?"). Teacher frustration arises because the latter should be, and needs to be, squelched; but a reasonable amount of the former must take place if classroom work is to proceed in an orderly way.

One classroom rule must be maintained at all times, no matter what: When the teacher is on his feet ready to talk, everybody else stops talking and listens. Not almost everybody, *everybody*. The teacher does not begin unless and until everybody listens and every eye is on him. (He returns this courtesy by exercising self-discipline in what he says, of course. He tries not to bore his students to intellectual and emotional jelly.)

Use all of the class time, every last shred of it. Keep the students working up until a minute or two before the bell rings. Allow only as much time as necessary for finding the page in the text, completing the exercise, handing in the papers, and so on.

As exasperating as such busywork may be to the teacher, most schools expect the roll to be checked every period. In a departmentalized school organization, alas, such a procedure is necessary for maintaining adequate control of truancy. The rigamarole of absence slips must be attended to, the gradebook marked, and the names of students cutting classes sent to the office. In our age of automation, it seems a rather flagrant waste of the teacher's time, but there it is.

By all means use your seating charts and conduct the roll-checking operation while the students are at work. No educational benefit whatever is realized when students listen to their classmates saying "here." It is very boring, and classroom buzz takes over in no time at all.

The buzz situation is hopeless only when the teacher isn't aware there is a problem. If he conducts classroom lectures and other activities against a constant undercurrent of student talking, he comes to accept this noise as the normal condition of the classroom. Almost without realizing it, he raises his voice in an effort to drown it out. He is comfortable in his illusion that he is "teaching," although few of his students actually ever hear a word he says. He wonders, year after year, why they always send him poor students.

The Borrowers

Collecting the small amounts of money, the pencils, the pens, and the textbooks that students are forever borrowing from you is fairly simple. Ask for collateral until the money is repaid or the pen or pencil returned. Collateral may be a ring, a watch, or the student's car keys—a shoe if he has nothing else. It must be an article the student won't be likely to leave unclaimed.

This sounds Simon Legree-ish, but, carried off in a spirit of good sportsmanship, there is no cause for resentment. Nobody knows better than the students themselves how easy it is to wander off with a borrowed pen, regardless of whose it is. If something of value has been left in hock, the pen will be returned. If not, you're likely never to see it again.

Be ready for the students who will come to your class-room unprepared to do school work at all—no pencil, no pen, no paper, no homework assignment, no textbook, nothing. These will be the students who are only there at all because the attendance officer threatened to drag the old man into court if his kid didn't go to school. All the student wants, he'll tell you, is to leave school and get a job as soon as he's old enough to quit legally. He'll probably go to his job every morning just as unprepared as he is for your class, if he's lucky enough to get a job; but this isn't your problem. If you say to him, "You poor dear misunderstood child," and give him free access to all the supplies he needs, he'll leave your cupboard as bare as the day it came from the factory. If you say, "Okay, Buster, so sit there and flunk," he'll generate disturbance and ultimately make a travesty of your class.

Always keep a supply of wastepaper from the ditto machine—sheets that came through the machine wrinkled, too faint, or with incorrect margins. Sometimes there are stacks of old forms the school's not using anymore. There's nothing wrong with writing on the back of such paper. Cut the 8½ x 11 sheets in half on the paper cutter and keep a quarter-inch stack in some regular place in the classroom for the use of students who don't have paper. Don't put out more than that or they'll take it to make confetti for the ball game. Don't put out good notebook or ditto paper or they'll take it to use in other classes or for brothers and sisters to use at *their* schools.

The no-pencil problem can be solved by keeping on hand some pencils that are good enough to make a readable page but so undesirable they won't be stolen. If you know a reading teacher on your faculty, ask him if he has any of those colored pencils that come in the reading laboratories. Very few reading teachers use them, and they just sit around. The students hate to use them, so they won't be stolen.

Never make it easy for a kid to flunk. Too many students choose this path, deliberate failure, to get even with their parents, with the school, or with the world in general. They're cutting off their noses to spite their faces, of course, and the greatest service you can do these immature and not-very-wise juveniles is to put every obstacle in the way of achieving that goal. Your time will be limited and you can't manage many obstacles, but you can take care of the paper-pencil-book thing.

Notes

There are several things you can do when you catch a student passing a note to another student when they're both supposed to be doing something else.

1. You can intercept the note and read it aloud to the class, realizing as you do that it may contain a raunchy comment or two about you!
2. You can intercept it, correct the spelling, and return it with a reprimand.
3. You can intercept it, tear it up, and drop it in the waste-basket.
4. If you want to be a real fiend, you can intercept it and do nothing at all. Tuck it in a pocket or the back of your gradebook until the end of the period, at which time you return it, unread, with no comment whatever.

Gum

Gum is sometimes forbidden in schools, both because teen-agers look and sound unpleasant when chewing it and because the wads of chewed gum are often disposed of between the pages of classroom books. (To remove without damaging the pages, take the book home with you and moisten the back of the stuck page with an ice cube. The chilled gum will fall loose.)

Another favorite repository is beneath the surface of school furniture. It can require a morning of a custodian's time to clean a well-encrusted desk of a year's residue of gum. Unfortunately, it requires much more than that of a teacher's time to enforce a no-gum rule, so nobody really wins the chewing gum fight but the people who make the stuff. If you must enforce it, the first two or three times you catch a student, tell him to wrap the wad in a piece of paper and drop it in the wastebasket. The fourth time, have him come around at noon or after school, give him a scraper, and make him scrape fifteen wads of gum off the undersides of the desks in your room. Fifth offense, thirty wads. Sixth offense, sixty wads. If you run out of gum for him to scrape off, borrow some well-encrusted desks from a neighboring classroom or move your operation to the library.

Snacks

School rules usually forbid eating in classrooms. A student can't concentrate on his food and his books at the same time. Moreover, bits of food attracts rats, mice, and insects. Students who nibble forbidden snacks in class will invariably keep the open box of candies, peanuts, or raisins in an easily-accessible pocket. When your back is turned, or even when it isn't, goodie-in-pocket quickly becomes goodie-in-mouth by exercise of some of the most skillful sleight of hand since Houdini. You might teach for years and never actually witness this transfer. What gives the game away is the smell. Does your nose tell you there are peanuts around? Licorice? Look over a few shoulders. Peep into a few chest pockets. You will see the box. Ask for the box. Tell the student he may have it back at the end of the period. Give it back to him at the end of the period.

There are really and truly students who eat no breakfast at home but buy a Coke and a doughnut at school to start the day on. They'll want to eat this impromptu meal in your home room or first period class. Don't permit it. Send the student outside in the hall to finish breakfast. Tell him that henceforth he is to get to school in time to finish eating outside the classroom before the bell rings.

But I've Got To Go

"May I go to the restroom?"

"No, sorry."

"But I've got to go."

"Why didn't you go before you came to class?"

"I didn't have time."

"Well, the bell will ring in twenty minutes or so and you'll have time then. If you'll remind me, I'll dismiss you a couple of minutes early."

You'll say this to a dozen different students before you will find one who remembers to remind you.

"But I can't wait. I've got to go *now*."

When a student is having stomach cramps, or when a female student is in sudden monthly distress, you'll know it. In the first instance, there's a funny pinched look around the mouth, and in both cases students have a bad case of jitters for fear the emergency might overwhelm them. It isn't hard to spot this. Let the jittery student go and don't argue.

You'll find you need to hold the line, though, against the student who simply becomes bored in class and wants to walk around for a little fresh air, who wants to smoke a cigarette, or who has made a date to meet the boy friend by the water fountain. In all secondary schools, classes change every hour or so, with five or ten minute breaks between each class. For any student to maintain the fiction that nature's calls can't be attended to during these once-an-hour intervals is rather flimsy. Even students with bona fide kidney trouble don't need more time than that!

How Fresh?

The dividing line between garden-variety rudeness ("Larry, you haven't put your name on your paper. How can I tell whose it is?" "Sorry about that, Chief."), which is as much a part of growing up as pimples, and insolence ("Fred, let's stop talking now and get to work." "I ain't ready yet."), which is a challenge to authority, is a fine one. A clear refusal to obey should be dealt with firmly and promptly. "Who asked if you were ready? Get to work."

The student who is merely "fresh" is never motivated by ill-will. On the contrary, this may be his somewhat gauche way of telling you he thinks you're all right. The easier, maybe even the wiser way, is to accept these little familiarities for what they are, a form of tribute, and forget it.

There are courageous teachers who sincerely feel one of the proper functions of the school is to teach good manners along with everything else. These brave souls have their work cut out for them. If you can manage to do it without short-circuiting your nervous system, fine. But don't be surprised if progress is slow. Whether you try or not, don't despair. One day in the future, it may be your good fortune to run into a twenty-five-year-old you knew as a disagreeable, wisecracking oaf at fourteen. You will be overwhelmed to see he has developed into a paragon of politeness and charm—social smile securely in place; "yes, sir," "no, sir"; articulate; helpful—all good things! Who taught him to act like that? Well, you probably did. As young people grow to adulthood, they model themselves after older adults they have known and admired. Since young people see more of their teachers than anybody else—in a few cases, even more than their parents—the educator bears a heavy responsibility. He must try especially hard to be a worthy model.

Cheating

It's doubtful that even students themselves realize the extent to which cheating goes on in a big high school. Perhaps it's just as well. There are standard ways that you can combat cheating:

1. All the time the students are taking an important test, be on your feet walking around the room—not through the middle of it, mind you, but around the periphery, looking in. Be alert for unauthorized papers of any kind; "tattooed" wrists and arms; and any unusual interest in shoes, cuffs, handbags, or wallets. Keep an especially close eye on the student who is keeping an especially close eye on you.
2. Let students know well in advance that anyone caught cheating on a test will fail the test. Stick to it, even if it's your pet-of-the-moment you must flunk and it nearly kills you.
3. Give tests that sample over-all comprehension, which are hard to prepare crib sheets for, rather than rote memory tests, which are easy to prepare crib sheets for. (Ask "Why did . . .?" questions rather than "When did . . .?" or "Who did . . .?" questions.)
4. Never give a test twice in exactly the same way. If you're giving the identical test all day long to five different classes, change one section of it slightly. Select a different topic for an essay question for each class, or give different classes the same questions in a different sequence.
5. Don't pass out test or exam sheets until each desk is cleared of everything but pencil or pen.

6. Arrange for at least a few themes or reports to be written in class under your supervision and turned in at the end of the period. This gives you a sample of the student's writing ability. Later, if he suddenly turns in something that looks suspiciously A-ish, you will have his C-ish work to consult for comparison.

7. Many English teachers have their students bring to class the books they're reporting on and write the reports while there. This gives the teacher an opportunity to go from student to student asking pertinent questions about the books to determine if they were actually read or if a friend merely loaned both book and plot résumé.

8. When you discover that answers have been written into exercises in books on the classroom shelves or in school-issued books, don't waste several hours of your good time erasing them; write in more answers of your own, all wrong. Warn the students that you did this.

9. Guard your answer keys with your life.

10. Guard your gradebook with your life, especially if you're teaching college-prep students.

School-issued Books

A dreary but necessary job the teacher must cope with is keeping up with school-provided textbooks, supplementary books on permanent loan to the classroom, lab equipment, art supplies, and shop tools. A fully-equipped classroom costs between $25,000 and $75,000. Ordinary use and deterioration gobble a large hunk of that investment every year. If, in addition, little hunks of it walk out the door daily and never come back, before long there won't be enough district money left to keep teachers' salaries up with the cost-of-living index—and we don't want that to happen, do we?

The best defense a teacher has against students who will not only steal him blind but deaf and dumb as well, is to know what is in his room. If certain items are *not* in his room, he needs to know who has them, how long they have been out of the room, when they are due back; and he has to see to it they *get* back.

Keep a sign-out list. A clipboard is fine. There should be a column for sign-out date, item, name of student, date due back, and check-in. All books should be numbered, and this number should be listed as well as the title. This is also important where several identical items of equipment are available in the classroom. For numbering books and equipment don't rely on a little gummed sticker that can easily be pulled off. Affix a steel tag with cement, if necessary.

It's as important to be rigorous about signing things back in as it is about signing them out. Demand that the student bring the item he has returned to you so you can check it in personally. Otherwise, three days later you will ask him about it and he'll say, "I brought it back yesterday." If he can find the item with its identifying number in the room and show it to you to prove he returned it, fine. But if he isn't able to, you are stalemated. Did he really bring it back? Did someone else walk off with it? Insist that an item is not considered "checked in" at all unless you check it in personally and put it back in its accustomed place.

And if the student doesn't return something he has signed out? Many won't. Then you nag (*see* page 49). When an item is signed out by a student and is not returned after reminding and reminding and reminding, and also when school debts are unpaid, the school may refuse to release any of the student's records until he has settled his obligations. Perhaps his high school diploma may be withheld until he has done this.

Psychologically, it's bad to have too much of something on hand in the classroom. The moral structure of the young seems to have a built-in Robin Hood component: it's wrong to steal from the poor but virtuous to steal from the rich. With no qualms of conscience at all, students will whittle away at your opulent treasure of books, art paper, wrenches, or scrap lumber, to relieve you of the bother of keeping up with all that stuff. If you don't have much, on the other hand, he'll tend to identify with you—he doesn't have much, either—and leave your things alone.

Keep reserve supplies under lock and key where students never see them, out of the room, if necessary. Maintain a small rotating collection of supplementary books that you can keep track of rather than a large collection that is sure to disappear as the months pass.

Collecting Debts

Like the embezzler who intends to pay the money back but doesn't, there are students who intend to return the book, pay for the tickets they checked out to sell, pay back the dollar they borrowed from the teacher, pay for the dress pattern ordered in home economics class, pay for the school photographs, but don't. Elementary schools have recourse to the parents in these situations; secondary schools, more interested in developing personal responsibility in young adults, hound them for the money.

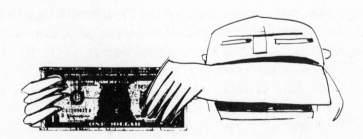

There is no drearier job. It runs something like this:

Day 1: "May I have your attention? Some of the students in our home room have turned in their picture money or the photographs they don't want to buy, but I still do not have envelopes from the following students: Avalon, Babson, Broderic, Chisholm, Davis, Dawson, Ghilarducci, Great-house, Hannon, Livermore, Roberts, Strum, Thomas, Trim-ble, Westover, White, and Yarbrough. Will you people whose names I read make it a point either to bring your photographs back or bring your money tomorrow?"

Day 2: "Some of you still haven't settled up for your photographs. I want to see the following people: Avalon, Broderic, Chisholm, Davis, Dawson, Ghilarducci, Hannon, Livermore, Roberts, Thomas, Trimble, Westover and Yar-brough.

"All right, Avalon, what's with you? Where are your pictures?"

"I guess I lost 'em."

"Have you looked for them at home?"

"Naw."

"You owe the photographer $2.50. When will you have the money?"

"I dunno. Pa don't get paid till next Wednesday."

"Next Wednesday. Let's see, that's October 7th. He gets paid October 7th, so you should have the money next day, October 8th. Will you write that date down here beside your name? October 8. And initial it, please. Thank you. I'll expect your money then. In the meantime, why don't you look around at home and see if you can't find them. . . . Broderic?"

"They're in my locker."

"What are they doing there?"

"I never took 'em home."

"Why not?"

"They was lousy."

"You never intended to buy any?"

"Lord, no."

"I wonder why you didn't turn them in three days ago?"

"I forgot."

"Go to your locker and get them now. . . . Chisholm?"

"I ain't got enough money to pay you now."

"How much money do you have now?"

"Only a buck and my lunch money."

"Your parents gave you the $2.50 and you spend $1.50 of it?"

"Naw. A guy stole it off me."

"Tell me about it."

"It was in P.E. My billfold was lying there and I came back and he was the only one in the room."

"When do you have P.E.?"

"Second period."

"You were here in home room first thing that morning with the $2.50 for the photographs before you even went to P.E. Why didn't you give me the money for your pic-tures while you had it?"

"I dunno." (Wasn't stolen at all. May have lost it in a crap game.)

"You'll have to ask your parents for the rest of the money or get a job and earn it."

"I can't ask them."

"If you don't pay, the school will ask them. How would you rather have them find out, from you or from us?"

"From me."

"In the meantime, pay the dollar you have. Can you bring the rest tomorrow?"

"I'll try."

"Don't try. Do it. Write the date down here beside your name and initial it."

The bell rings, home room period is over, and you have not yet had a chance to talk to Davis, Dawson, Hannon, Livermore, Roberts, Thomas, Westover, or Yarbrough. Ghilarducci and Trimble are absent. Broderic has not yet returned from his locker.

Day 3: Broderic brings his photographs from his locker. Westover brings in his money. Chisholm has dug up $1.50 from somewhere—maybe he won it back in another crap game. Don't ask. Hannon volunteers that he will have his money on Friday. You interrogate Davis, Hannon and Ghilarducci, who is back. Dawson and Trimble are absent.

Day 4: You collect from Davis. Dawson returns with her money. Ghilarducci and Trimble are absent. You talk to Livermore, Roberts, Thomas and Yarbrough.

Day 5: Hannon and Yarbrough bring in money and photographs, respectively. Although Thomas promised to pay, he hasn't yet, so you talk to him again. Ghilarducci and Trimble are absent.

Day 6: Avalon's father has been paid, and Avalon brings his $2.50. Livermore has made arrangements to work his money out at $1.00 per week in the cafeteria. Roberts returns his photographs, which his mother discovered under his books when she cleaned his room. You talk to Thomas again, who is still giving you promises and that's all. You have received a notice that Trimble has been expelled from school. Ghilarducci is absent.

Day 7: Thomas has now promised to have his money on four successive days, but still hasn't produced it. You turn in both his name and Ghilarducci's to the vice-principal, who will also take over with Livermore. That finishes up the picture money until next year.

There aren't many ways out of this collection situation. It's true that with something like the photographs you can operate on a cash-and-carry basis, especially with students

who have proven themselves poor credit risks before. However, suppose everybody is selling peanuts to make money
for the band uniforms. Very few of the students' neighbors,
brothers, or even mothers are going to give up the money
for the peanuts until they see the peanuts. After all, they
know the kids even better than you do! So if you refuse
to part with the merchandise until you get the money from
the students, your home room won't sell enough peanuts
to feed a spider monkey three days; and when they put the
sales figures up on the big chart in the hall, your home room
will be the lowest and class spirit will fly out the window.
So you're damned if you do and damned if you don't.

Often, one suspects, it becomes a kind of game with certain kinds of students to see who can hold out longest
without paying their bills. Professional bill collectors contend with the same phenomenon with the public at large.
Private business enjoys the delicious privilege of refusing
credit to poor risks, but the public school seldom enjoys such
a prerogative.

Successful hounding requires perseverance, patience, and
most annoying of all, time that could be spent teaching the
student something more interesting than that he must meet
his monetary obligations. Due to the large amount of classroom time that can melt away while the teacher exhorts
laggard students to settle up, one seldom sees money change
hands in the classroom proper anymore. The general practice is for these transactions to take place during the home
room period or through the office.

The Pep Rally

There are up days and down days in the pulsing life of a
school. Monday is depressive; Friday is manic. The Friday
before a vacation is hyper-manic. So are the classes immediately preceding a pep rally or a school assembly.

Because of the competition for the students' attention, it's a temptation to throw away these times and go through the motions of teaching in a wooden and unenthusiastic way, or perhaps have "supervised study" and not teach at all.

Resist this temptation. Your students are in school for what goes on in class. The pep rallies and assemblies are the head on the beer—morale raisers and school spirit builders. If you compromise this position, you are letting down both your students and your school. Try to time your best, not your worst, lesson plans for assembly days. Wear your best suit that day, your brightest smile, and deliver your most scintillating lecture.

The Disadvantaged

Scarcely a teacher in a high school classroom, man or woman, is without a tale about the time, back when he first started teaching, that the first black-leather-jacket kid— perhaps Negro, Mexican-American, or Indian—slouched into his classroom, hands in pockets, to all appearances spoiling for a fight.

To one who has never dealt with culturally deprived (*i.e.*, poor) people before, they offer an awesome prospect. They are beings from another world. Their values are different, their customs are different, and their modes of living are almost totally alien. Many criminals come from their ranks, and the opportunity to become a criminal as a way of life is presented to each of them daily. Yet only a small minority are, or will become, criminals. The majority will resist the drift towards crime because they have guts, character, and common sense in no less degree than human beings of any other socio-economic background.

When these people enter the middle-class world of the school, they encounter one of two attitudes, hostility or bleeding-hearts pampering. Neither of these attitudes do anything towards reducing the already heavy burdens they bear with them to school. What they do need is to be treated exactly as everybody else. Ignore the black jacket, the processed hair, the moustache, the tattoo, the fright-wig hair style, and the skin-tight skirt. As for the Cleopatra eye make-up, you do the young lady no favor when you demand she remove it. Her boy friend thinks it makes her look sexy. Since she must induce him to marry her by the time she's seventeen or be considered a failure among her own people, this is a good thing for him to think.

There is no need to placate, berate, or to attempt to solve the problems of the poor in your classes. All you need to do is teach them. Armed with knowledge, they will be able to solve their problems far better than you can.

The Low Point

Someday you will draw a class that will make you wish you'd stayed on shore and cut bait. Let's hope you don't, but you will. In this class there will be a higher proportion than usual of compulsive showoffs, authority-challengers, big talkers, and general grandstanders. Typically, it will be a big class, thirty-five or more. In spite of the application of every rule you or anybody else can think of, it will be impossible to get this class to pursue a classroom discussion, watch a film, or work on a project without disintegrating into wrangling, joking, chalk-throwing, shoving disorder.

Look for trouble first in the material you're using to teach. Is it too difficult or too easy? Is the range of ability in the class extremely wide, so that what is too easy for the better students is too difficult for the slower ones? If so, you may be forced to group the class. Did these students have a similar course of study the year before, presented in much the same way? Perhaps they aren't convinced what you're offering them is worthwhile. What's needed is either a new approach or a selling job. In the meantime, it will take you two or three days to get a proper analysis of the situation. To enable you to keep the class under control while you stall for time, there are two standard gimmicks: (1) Have the students take turns reading aloud from the textbook, and (2) have them copy something from the chalkboard.

If, upon completing your analysis, you find that none of the suggested complications exist and that you have nothing more nor less than a giant-economy-size discipline problem on your hands, you will be compelled to change your teaching method entirely. As much as it will hurt your pride to do so, you will have to give up teaching and begin to baby-sit.

Cut your lectures to a minimum. Plan the whole period, every day, for seatwork of some kind for this class. There will be no films, no phonograph records, no class discussions, and no oral reports. The schoolwork for that class will consist of reading and written work—alone, at their desks. This will give you a ton of papers to grade. Don't grade them all. Take a few at random; check them and return them the next day. (Irregular reinforcement schedules; no student ever knows when his paper will be checked. More effective than checking every paper, anyway.)

While students are working at their desks, patrol the room. Walk. No student is to leave his seat without permission, even to sharpen a pencil. Don't talk aloud yourself and don't allow the students to do so. Hold whispered conversations with them at their seats about their work.

Don't make a point of this shift to seatwork. Don't comment, just do it. Before long, students in this class will compare notes with students of your other classes and discover they're missing out on the goodies.

"Why didn't *we* get to see the film yesterday?"

"You can't handle it."

"What's that supposed to mean?"

"It means you can't handle it. A teacher must adapt his lesson plans to the needs of the students. When the students are mature enough, the teacher can do many different things —show films, have debates, things like that. The more mature the students, the more flexible the teacher's lesson plans can be."

"Then you mean you don't think we're mature. Is that it?"

"Well, let's say I think there are some basic things you people need to learn about proper behavior before you're ready to do things my other classes do."

This will arouse squawks, grumbling, cries of "foul." When the protests become loud enough, it's time for your coup.

"Would you like me to show you a film so that you can see what I mean?"

The day you show the film, have a little surprise for them. You'll have obtained a tape recorder and an hour's worth of blank tape. You're going to get the evidence down in some tangible form so there'll be no argument about their "maturity." If you've played your cards right, they'll show you (with the tape to prove it) that you're wrong.

Vandalism

One afternoon after the students have gone, while making your final check of the room before going home yourself, you will suddenly be aware of a Playboy-type picture carved on one of the students' desks. You'll wonder how long it's been there and which little monster did it. Well, the little monster who did it was the one who was sitting there. Consult your seating charts.

There are six periods in the school day, which gives you at least six different suspects—maybe. The desks aren't nailed down; the carved one could have been moved from another location while you were on duty in the hall.

You may become involved in a day or two of private questioning before you locate the artist. Remember, the students who were seated in that part of the room won't tell you who did it. But they'll tell you who *didn't* do it, and you can discover the culprit by the process of elimination.

Once you have unearthed your Michelangelo, get the shop teacher to supply you with sandpaper, stain, and varnish and teach him the rudiments of furniture refinishing after school. If he rides a school bus, have him come during the noon hour. *Do not have him do this during class.*

Readers familiar with Skinnerian psychology will see the booby trap in this procedure. The boy or girl hostile enough to carve on furniture may feel rewarded, not punished, by the annoyance he causes the teacher. With such pleasurable reinforcement, he is more likely to repeat the offense than not. This will be the very student you need to pay attention to and work with when he does something *right*, not when he does something *wrong*. But justice must outweigh Skinner. If a student damages public property, he must be compelled to undo the damage—if, indeed, it can be undone.

It's possible to at least accommodate Skinner by shifting the focus of the situation. The "punishment" aspect can be abandoned once the teacher and the student are alone with the job. The session then becomes a matter-of-fact teaching-learning situation in which the student successfully learns something constructive and is commended for having done a good job. This way, the pleasure the student derives from being the center of the teacher's attention is not in witnessing a pyrotechnical display of the teacher's anger, but in assuming his proper role as a student and in succeeding as a student.

Most state laws stipulate that the student's parents are liable for damage to school property. If the mutilation is so extensive a professional is required to fix it, the vice-principal should be asked to have a look before anything is said to the student. Whether the damage is extensive or not, file a written report about it.

Paradoxically, vandalism is most effectively prevented by a moderate discipline policy. As far as schoolwork is concerned, establishing high standards and maintaining steady pressure on the students to come up to the standards are necessary if learning is to take place. Assignments must be turned in properly prepared and on time, and the lab workbook must be kept up to date. The business of the school is, after all, learning, and this is business to be taken seriously.

On the other hand, Horace Mann won't stir in his grave if there's a scrap of paper on the floor, or if students don't address the teacher as "sir" or "ma'am." The teacher who is rigidly authoritarian or hostile, or both, builds up a formidable reservoir of repressed anger in his students. This anger will find release someplace, you may be sure. Either the students will turn on each other like a pack of voracious wolves, or they will do other things—carve up the furniture, for instance.

Pictures of Teacher

There will inevitably be the episode, not necessarily vandalism, when you find a picture of yourself—yes, you, teacher!—in a textbook, tacked to the bulletin board, or peeping at you from between the covers of a student's notebook. It will be hideously unflattering. The student may have drawn it after he flunked a test, or after you said something nice about a student he felt to be his rival for your esteem—sibling rivalry is almost as common in the classroom as it is in the home.

When you come upon this, you might exclaim with mild pleasure, "Oh, look! Another picture for my collection! Did you do this, Tommy? Please sign it for me, will you?" and so on. Put it away in your desk drawer and—well, why *not* start a collection?

Suppose it's on the chalkboard. "Ooh" and "ah" a bit but don't appear anxious to erase it. Within fifteen or twenty minutes after having first discovered it, invent some pretext to use that particular section of the chalkboard so you can erase it and put up something else. Don't leave it there. If a parent drops by to say hello, it will be hard to explain.

Suppose the portrayal is so sadistic or lewd it makes you want to find a quiet corner and vomit. Raise your eyebrows, say "Hm," and then put it away in your desk and continue with your teaching as though nothing had happened. Never mention it in class again. Ask the vice-principal about it. You may have a psychopath on your hands. If he doesn't think so, take the picture home, burn it, and forget it.

Your Audio-visual Assistant

Damaged audio-visual equipment is seldom a result of deliberate classroom vandalism. It is usually the result of the youthful exuberance of untrained operators who think they are quite able to operate the equipment without the teacher being on hand to supervise. A thorough scolding is all that's called for here, even though the damage an over-enthusiastic student can do to a motion picture projector or to a film may require hours for the technicians in the AV department to repair.

If the guilty student is eager to operate the equipment, why not use him properly? Bring him in for a couple of training sessions and make him your regular projectionist.

Theft

If an article of value ($5.00 or over) or money ($2.00 or over) has been stolen from your classroom, say and do nothing until you get somebody else—preferably the vice-principal, in the room with you. Don't let anyone leave but the victim, whom you send for help.

There are several reasons why you shouldn't handle matters like this alone, the main one being that you don't have eyes in the back of your head. Another reason is that if an expensive article is at stake, the parents must be notified and the vice-principal needs to be able to talk to them from first-hand evidence. Another reason is that he will have experience in dealing with many such incidents before. He will know the students and their shortcomings so well from years past that he will have narrowed your list of suspects to three or four before he arrives at your door. Students who have made trouble in the past, alas, tend to make trouble in the present and future.

When the vice-principal or another teacher has arrived on the scene, line the students up against the wall and have them empty pockets and purses on the desks. Watch the entire group while the vice-principal goes from student to student, or vice versa. If you try to make this student-by-student search on your own, the hot item can be disposed of behind your back—hidden in a notebook, shoe, coat pocket, etc. Don't be so naive as to expect the "good" students to squeal on the "bad" ones. According to the teen-age code, adults must spear their own fish or go hungry.

If and when the missing article is found, the offending student is escorted to the office. There, the vice-principal takes over. If it's money, two or three students in the group may be carrying more than would normally be expected. They are asked to stand to one side. All of them but one will have explanations that can be verified by telephone calls to their parents. But one won't, unless his parents cover for him. Sometimes this happens, too.

Suppose money disappears and the theft isn't discovered until after the students have left the room? Notify the vice-principal at once.

In the matter of school thefts, there is always an important factor working for the members of the school staff trying to find the culprit and against the culprit himself. The motive behind virtually any theft is the desire for status. The thief wants to have a finer jacket, a more handsome watch, or to spend more money on snacks. Since the very friends he wants to impress are there, in the school, mingling hourly with the same persons who are out to nail his hide to the wall, he can't very well attract the attention of one without also attracting the attention of the others. The kid can't resist flashing around whatever it was he stole; the wrong people see him, and *zap!* Many outside as well as inside crimes are solved this way. The Sharp Dresser might be arrayed in the take from last week's pawnshop burglary, and the Big Spender may be spreading the benefits of a recent service station heist. As pointed out previously, the vice-principal is in close touch with the police at all times.

When a student flashes a roll of bills or an article you know is beyond the means of either himself or of his family, ask about it. If he says he earned the money, ask him where. If he says he bought the article at a store, ask to see the sales slip. Perhaps he can't produce one. If he does, and the hand-writing on the slip looks suspiciously like the student's own, thank him noncommittally. Get word to the vice-principal.

Within a short time, you'll get to know all your students so well you'll notice unusually flashy items of clothing, jewelry, etc., that turn up unexpectedly in their possession. Don't wonder about them in silence. Ask where they came from. "Dad bought it for me in L.A." "Yesterday was my birthday." Responses such as these are fine. The four answers that should set bells ringing are: "I found it," "I borrowed it," "Louise and I traded," and "Marian sold it to me." Let's take them one at a time:

1. "*I found it.*" "If you found it, give it to me and I'll see it gets to the Lost and Found Department in the office where it belongs." "But I *found* it!" "Then it doesn't be-long to you, does it? Give it to me." Take it and turn it in at the office. Too often, Student A casts covetous eyes upon an especially attractive item brought to school by Student B. He bides his time, waiting for Student B to walk away from it momentarily so he can "find" it. Student B may put down his things, walk across the room to get a book, and return to discover someone has "found" the article that was

on his desk when he left. Student B doesn't know this, of course. All Student B knows is it's gone. *No finding* sounds like a silly rule. Yet, if you insist that no "found" articles may be kept but must be turned in to the central Lost and Found Department, a lot of grief may be avoided.

2. "*I borrowed it.*" "From whom?" "Jane Hughes. She's a friend of mine." "Does she know you borrowed it?" "We're friends, I tell you. She doesn't care." "You're not to lend or borrow things from classmates. Give it to me. Tell Jane I have it. Send her to me and I'll give it to her." "But I just *borrowed* it!" "And I shall return it for you. Give it to me." You may know Jane Hughes. However, if you don't . . . "And by the way, be sure to tell Jane to bring some identification with her." The more resistance you encounter in this situation, the more certain you can be that Jane will never show. There may be no Jane at all; the name may be a fiction. If there is a Jane, being unaware she lent anything, the last person to tell her is going to be the "borrower" who no longer has the "borrowed" item! Take it to the Lost and Found. If Jane by any chance does appear, give her a stern word of warning about lending her personal possessions and see she gets her property back. In secondary schools, where a student may know the combinations to several friends' lockers as well as his own, the temptation to "borrow" an article without the knowledge of the owner may be irresistable. *No borrowing* isn't a silly rule, either.

3. "*Louise and I traded.*" "Tell me about it." Write it all down. Full names. Home rooms. Description of items. Technically innocent theft can occur when Student A trades her $2.95 red woolly sweater to Student B for Student B's $29.95 imported cashmere jacket. Though the swap may be fair in the eyes of both students, it definitely will not be fair in the eyes of Student B's parents.

4. "*Marion sold it to me.*" "Tell me about it." Write it all down. Student B's parents aren't going to be any happier if their daughter sells the cashmere jacket to a fellow student

for fifty cents than they'll be about a swap. But the money factor here is a little different. As has been said elsewhere, students are people. Like people everywhere, they are forever getting themselves into jams about money. Student B's parents have given her the money to pay her club dues at school. She has frittered it away on candy and potato chips for herself and her friends. The deadline arrives for paying the club dues. To forgo the club is unthinkable; all her friends are in it. She dares not confess her plight to her parents and face their anger, so she liquidates some of her assets at a fraction of their true value and tells her parents the articles were "stolen" or "lost." Well, in a sense they were, which is why *no buying* and *no trading* aren't silly rules, either.

In cases of inter-student "buying" and "trading," the thing to do is take down all the information and turn it over to the vice-principal. Five will get you ten the parents will phone wanting to know what kind of school you're running over there. (They always want to know what kind of school you're running over there.) The vice-principal will appreciate having the information readily available.

You will note the emphasis on preventive action throughout this chapter. Teaching, not policing and crime detection, is the top-priority business of the school. The more minutes you devote to crime prevention, the more hours you'll save on crime detection. Shakedowns, searches, and interrogations are unbelievably time consuming. When a serious felony has been committed, an entire morning can disappear and still the missing article won't be found. If it is found, the parents of the offender or perhaps the juvenile authorities must be summoned, and so it goes on and on and on.

Love and the Teacher

Nearly all students, at one time or another in their school lives, get a crush on a teacher. Sooner or later, a student will get a crush on you. When this happens, you'll know it. The onset is as obvious as a skunk in the room. The kid looks ill, hangs around all the time, and leaps to do your bidding.

Pleasant though this may be in some cases, it isn't normal.

The teacher should gently ease the student over his crisis so there will be as little traumatic aftereffect as possible.

There are a number of ways to accomplish this. If you have a wife, say nice things about her frequently. A husband, ditto. Keep framed pictures of the kiddies on your desk. If you have none of these assets, invent a mythical true love from another city to whom you are very devoted. This person phones you long distance and possesses unusually fine talents, intellect, etc., all of which you happen to mention in class or to groups of your students out of class.

If you are past thirty, you can say things about your age. "When I was a little boy, Grandfather took me to hear Lincoln at Gettysburg, bla bla bla." Talk about your pills, your allergies, your diet; bumble around a little. Use 1930's slang, or to kill even the most ardent puppylove, use 1960's slang like somebody who grew up in the 1930's and is trying hard.

So much for the student who has a crush on the teacher. There is also, alas, the teacher who gets a crush on the student. Many generalizations are risky, but this one isn't. A teacher should never, never, *never* allow himself (or herself) to become physically attracted to *any* student.

To consciously yield to such a temptation is to invite in-
volvement in situations that are unethical, unprofessional—
and insane. To yield unconsciously is worse. The band
director invites the talented little blonde flutist to come
after school for extra coaching alone in the bandroom.
("That girl has a real concert-grade talent if only I can develop it.") The faculty sponsor of the school newspaper
works with the brilliant and lovely editor until long after
dark to get out the next issue of the paper. ("Linda and I
can get more done alone in five minutes than we can with
all those kids in two hours.") The math teacher undertakes
psychotherapy with his nymphomaniac, straight-F student.
("She needs help.")

Men are by no means the only ones who are subject to
this kind of poor judgment. The female teacher who tells
dirty jokes to her male students, who can't resist stroking
hard young biceps, is paying a high price in prestige for her
innocent expressions of camaraderie.

The aftertaste is bitter. Once established in the minds of
parents at home, a reputation for lechery is still alive and
kicking long after the teacher has become wiser.

Male teachers are fair game for either the nervous female
student who thinks she is being pursued and isn't, or for the
aggressive female who consciously wishes to be pursued
but isn't.

The nervous female invents things. "Mr. Smith has been
making passes at me for a month. If he doesn't stop, I'm
going to tell my father." Her entire stock of evidence might
amount to the fact that Mr. Smith moved her to the front
row (so she wouldn't talk so much), and one day when she
was examining a runner that unexpectedly popped just
above her knee, she glanced up and noticed that Mr. Smith's
face was pink (because he was stifling a sneeze). Yet from
this meager lode of reality, her imagination will mine leers,
intimate caresses, and whispered invitations.

Girls with many friends of both sexes don't do this kind of thing. Normally, it's the unwanted little urchin who turns a male teacher's simple request into a lewd proposition.

The aggressive female is different. She knows what she wants—to seduce that attractive man—and she arranges things so she'll be likely to get what she wants. The male teacher may be unaware of what is in her mind until he finds himself in a nightmarish tête-à-tête with her. She may begin to fondle him or undress. "Alone at last," she breathes in his ear. He may stammer in bewilderment or bellow in rage, depending on his temperament and the degree of his indignation. In either case, the fat is in the fire. In no time at all, he is learning once again about the fury of a woman scorned.

Several days later, in a hearing before the school board or in a courtroom, the teacher's fate will rest on this girl's histrionic talent. Bolstered by her own rage and hurt feelings at being rejected, she will by that time have come to believe her own lies and her histrionic talent will be impressive indeed. And who, other than the teacher himself, will know for certain she's lying?

When it comes to School Sex, two things will do the teacher in: privacy and time. If there is no privacy, there is no opportunity for a student to force improper issues herself or to claim the teacher forced them. If curriculum or counseling demands are such that a teacher must be alone with a student, the classroom or office door should be open. Or, if the hall is deserted, the interview might be conducted during a stroll to the office. If the teacher furnishes school-to-home transportation after the club meeting, a student of the same, not the opposite, sex, should be taken home last.

Of supreme importance is the need to act quickly when, having inadvertently given the student the opportunity, the teacher realizes he is being approached too familiarly. "No! No! Please don't tell anyone. Dear God! Please don't

tell anyone. My father will beat me! He'll call me a tramp
and kick me out of the house! It won't happen again, I
swear!!" All such hysterical pleas, promises, and explanations must be ignored no matter how brutal such behavior
may seem at the time. The teacher's career—not only his
job at that particular school, you understand, his career as
an educator—is in grave jeopardy. He should summon, in
order of preference or availability, the principal, the vice-
principal, the dean of boys, the dean of girls, the counselor,
the school nurse, the principal's secretary, another teacher
or teachers, any or all secretaries, the police, the fire department, the girl's parents, the juvenile authorities, the civil
defense people, or the S.P.C.A. He desperately needs wit-
nesses of equal or higher authority there, on the spot, at
that time, to have the thing out in the open before the
student has a chance to assuage her lacerated pride by inventing a story that will put her in a more flattering light.

Even then, there will be distortions of the truth. ("He
grabbed me by the shoulder.") But they will be as sheerest
gauze compared with the elaborate tapestry of false charges
the teacher will face if a third party isn't brought in until
a week later, a day later, or even an hour later. ("He ripped
my clothes off and said if I didn't do what he wanted, he'd
see I never got my high school diploma and neither would
my kid brother.")

Throughout the entire episode, should it drag on for
agonizing weeks or only for merciful minutes, the teacher's
ablest defender and advisor will be his principal. Experience
and a cool head are needed, and the principal will be more
likely than anybody else to have both. It will be the principal's intention to keep his school free of scandal if at all
possible. He will be reluctant to believe privately, and even
more reluctant to admit publicly, that there are persons on
his staff who are capable of unethical conduct. He will wish
to discourage malicious attacks on male members of the

school staff (including himself) by oversexed female students. He will also be loath to hire and break in a new teacher in the middle of the school year.

Violence

More rare even than the sex things, will be the occasion when you are done bodily harm by a student or students. In ninety per cent of America's schools, you can forget this threat. It won't come up. In schools where there has been a history of such incidents, the experience of other teachers or of the principal will be valuable to you. There may be uniformed policemen on duty at all times, and there may be a regular school procedure to follow in case you are jumped by a group of students. State laws enter into the situation. It isn't a matter of simple self-defense, as though you were attacked in a bar or on the street by other adults. These are juveniles. You have been entrusted with their care, and special laws apply—different laws in different states. Better ask.

Many classrooms are equipped with a two-way intercom system. Often, teachers are suspicious of this equipment because it enables administrators to listen in on their classes at any time and they feel they are being spied on. But there is another side of the coin; the equipment is there to protect them in an emergency. When you need help, buzz the office.

Another thorny but extremely rare problem is the student who becomes loud and abusive, shouting epithets and obscenities at the teacher. He won't shut up and he won't get out. What do you do? Buzz the office or send a student for help. You may not need to. If the student is loud enough, teachers in adjoining classrooms will come to your aid and help remove him bodily, if necessary. If a student has lost control to such a point you simply don't know what he will do, don't walk out and leave your other students there at his mercy. If you're afraid he might carve you up, there is also a possibility that he may carve up some of the other students while he's at it. Summon help, but stay there.

Both in the sex matter and in the case of violence in the classroom, it is to the teacher's interest to put himself in the hands of his principal, tell him exactly what happened, and do exactly what he says. The principal will probably tell the teacher not to discuss the matter with anyone else. That's the best advice of all. Let him handle it.

four

Student Stereotypes

"That kid is a pest!" says Teacher A to Teacher B. "All he wants is attention."

If Teacher A would only reflect a moment, he'd realize that's all Akhnaton wanted, or Charlemagne, or Madame Curie, or Thomas Jefferson, or Helen Keller. Is wanting attention bad? Heavens, no! Man would have foundered in the morass of his own folly centuries ago if it hadn't been for the visionaries, revolutionaries, and just plain crackpots who wanted attention and went about getting it in constructive ways.

Many of your students, alas, will go about getting it in inappropriate ways. It will become part of your task not to discourage the boy who paints blue daisies on his face, but to handle him in such a way that he may one day write an award-winning film script. (Creative artists of this caliber are few and far between!)

This chapter will be devoted to a discussion of stereotypes the teacher is likely to encounter in his classes, to-

71

gether with suggestions for resolving the problems typically presented by them. The same convention will be observed in discussing these students as has been employed in refer-ring to the teacher throughout this book, i.e., using the masculine gender. You should by no means assume from this that boys are troublemakers and girls aren't. Such is scarcely the case, although some categories are likely to be more heavily weighted toward one sex than the other.

Gigglers, for example, are usually girls, and there are possibly more female than male floaters, because they make liberal use of female problems to get out of class. On the other hand, Cliff Hanger I will nearly always be a boy, but Cliff Hanger II may more often be a girl.

Whether it's Robert or Roberta, Steve or Stephanie, how-ever, you will meet a goodly number of these stereotypes your first month in the classroom, and the rest before your first year is over.

The Clown

Every class of twenty-five or more will have a Clown. When he misbehaves, which is frequently, he does so in such a way you are sure to catch him and punish him. As a last resort, he will even point out to you what he did wrong and plead with you to punish him!

There is a streak of masochism in his make-up. He never wins. He arranges things so he won't. He gets his kicks from losing, from being the "stupid" one in the group, the butt of all the jokes.

What he needs from you, specifically, is your good-natured jibe before he can settle down happily to work. It's not the same if you kid him in private. There must be an audience.

Insulting this kid from time to time will keep his mischief in check but it won't help him to overcome his handicap, which, if allowed to pursue its course unchecked, will put him behind bars someday. He must be brought to see the value of satisfying his need for ridicule by means of an appropriate surrogate while reserving for his person the dignity which is his right as a human being.

In schoolwork, he might be channeled into dramatic comedy parts including Punch and Judy shows. He should do well in English with first-person-singular narrative in which the first-person-singular is a bumpkin of outlandish proportions. Comic dance, tumbling, trampoline acts, cartooning might answer. Another character *whom he has created* must be the fall guy, thus freeing him to work for, rather than against, his own best interests.

The Malingerer

This youngster is very hard on the nerves. He is a whiner, and usually a hypochondriac as well. He will have a bottomless reservoir of reasons why he can't do his homework, read the chapter, find something on the map, or do calisthenics. "Poor me," he says. "I am a victim of my weak constitution, bad eyes, poor education, crowded home, bad-tempered father, the welfare department, that mean teacher I had last year, mildew on my liver—you name it."

His goal is to squeeze from you every possible drop of sympathy. He may succeed for a while. He has had years of practice in sympathy-getting and has become proficient at it. You will wonder how he got that way until you meet his parents at the first P.T.A. meeting. After that, you'll know. They're that way, too.

This kid will nail you early, the first day. You are a fresh, untapped source of sympathy, and his eyes will mist over in happy anticipation. But don't go along with it. Tell him with a brisk smile that you can't do anything about his past troubles. You are there to help him learn so he may have fewer troubles in the future. If he suffers from poor health, all the more reason to study hard so he can overcome his handicap in the future when he must get a job. Do everything you can to get work of some kind out of this student. And when you get it, give him a warm smile of respect and commend him. Brush off his excuses, but never fail to commend his accomplishments. His accomplishments will probably be awful, just awful; but if he persists in his attempts to do his school work, his work will improve. You must have faith that this will happen and make him have faith it will happen. What you're primarily interested in is getting him to *do* something so he'll stop bellyaching about why he *can't* do it.

You won't reform the Malingerer all by yourself. Forget that. It would take far more than one teacher far more than one year to perform that miracle! But you can get him off your neck in your class. And who knows? You may actually succeed in teaching him something!

The Timeserver

This fellow is a lot like the Malingerer, but he presents a more complex problem. The Malingerer has at least bestirred himself to get something, sympathy. As long as there's a spark, a desire for something, no matter how sick the some-thing may be, you can direct this desire, encourage it, and perhaps come up with worthwhile results. But the Time-server doesn't want sympathy. He doesn't want anything. He just sits there. He is an inert mass of programmed ham-burger. He has been wired to get up and leave when the bell rings and, perhaps, answer rollcall, but little else. He almost never misbehaves actively, although he may take a nap from time to time. He rarely talks to anyone, least of all to you. He may be in your class a month before you hear him utter a sentence.

He isn't afraid he'll flunk. On the contrary, he is quite sure he will flunk, because he more often flunks than not. He has given up, and in his case it was probably the only sensible way to deal with an environment he could neither conform to nor change.

In any problem with a student, the less emotionally in-volved you allow yourself to become, the better off both of you will be, but particularly is this true in the case of the Timeserver. He, of all problem students, will be most likely either to infuriate you or to break your heart. His disinterest in you, school, books, and education is complete and bone deep.

Until you have time to find out more about him, leave him alone. Be pleasant. Speak to him just as you would to any other student. You need to research this student thoroughly before you make a move, so don't make any until you've asked not one or two, but several people about him. If there's any danger of borderline psychosis, you don't want to be the one to shove him over the line. Most of your in- formation will come from his counselor and other teachers, but oblique questioning of a few students who know him well may also help.

Is he mentally ill? Has he been referred to the school psychoanalyst? When? Was there treatment? For how long? With what results? Is there mental illness in his family? Does he act the same way outside of school as in it? Is he this way in all classes, including P.E. and shop? If not, you've got a fighting chance. How have other teachers handled him and what were the results?

His school records in the counselor's office should indicate how long he's been the way he is. When did he become a straight-F student? If he "gave up" within the last year or so, you may still snap him out of it. If it's gone on for three or more years or if he'll soon be of legal age to quit school or both, you're licked on the education end—but you may still be able to use him as a teacher's aide in your class.

Most important of all, is his behavior truly what it ap- pears to be, total demoralization, or is it a teacher-baiting device? It will be easy to determine this from the other teachers. Is he after peace at any price, or is he after a fight at any price? It is the answer to this question that will give you your cue in handling him.

If there is a history of mental disturbance, or even a suspicion anywhere that there might be such a condition, leave him alone. Smile at him. Perhaps once a week when the other students are working at their seats, you might quietly go to him and, in a whisper, invite him to do what the other students are doing. Don't order him; invite him.

If you're lucky and actually get work out of this student, say to him privately, "I was glad to see you turned in a paper yesterday, Robert. I'll bet it wasn't as bad as you thought it would be. Would you like me to show you the ones you got right?" Not *wrong*, notice; right. If you only talk about the right ones, soon he'll begin to wonder on his own about the wrong ones and either ask you about them or fix them up himself. Don't gush. Phony praise is worse than none at all.

If he doesn't respond to this tack, see if you can find magazines that interest him, or books. If you have a book table at the back of the room, let him sit there regularly. Be kind to him. Put things he might like where he can find them. And leave him alone.

If your research indicates, however, that this student is merely testing you to see how much you'll put up with, more pressure is called for; and you'll have to keep applying it over a long period of time—probably for the entire year.

Oddly enough, if this student weighs 200 pounds and you weigh 110 pounds, you have an advantage. But if the student weighs 200 and you weigh 180, you have no advantage. Don't ask me why. Maybe it has something to do with roles. Little people with a lot of gumption can push big lugs around and the big lugs love it and big, muscle-bound types can push runts around and the runts love it, but when the weight balance is close enough to leave doubt about who's the "big guy" and who's the "little guy," a contest develops. If you're near the same size, don't push or shove, *lean gently*.

Having been forewarned on this score, you should be forewarned on another. The hardest way to handle any discipline problem is to let it develop into an eyeball-to-eyeball "you will," "I won't," "you will," "I won't" dispute. All this proves is who can yell the loudest. Anyway, whether the student will or won't shouldn't be part of the issue at all. Assume from the outset that he will; the only matter in doubt is how well and to what extent.

Once you have determined that your Timeserver is not a borderline psychotic and there may be hope you can do something with him, see to it he is supplied with a textbook next time he comes to class. He won't have one with him. Give him one from the classroom supply. You'll also have to give him paper and pencil from the classroom supply. Find the right page for him. Gently explain to him in a few words what the class is doing. Treat him as you would your invalid kid brother whom you're fond of and want to take care of. Conduct your class as usual but keep coming back to his seat to see if he needs help. "You'll need to number down the side of the page, Al. Here, let me show you." "Would you like me to read that first question for you?"

No sarcasm is called for—no nasty innuendos, no asides to the other students in the class. You are dealing with an educationally crippled student who needs a lot of help. Your solicitude will begin to hurt his pride after a while, and he'll do something on his own to get kindly old you off his back.

Check his paper for him, what there is of it, right there at his seat. Let him see what he did right and explain what he did wrong. If you gave him a grade at all it would prob-ably have to be an F, so don't give him one. Confine your praise to a businesslike "good."

Next day, repeat the routine. Teach the kid "by hand" until he's operating on his own steam. If his work continues to be so poor he'd get F's if you gave him grades, don't give him any, ever. Explain at the office that you are tutoring this student because he has special learning problems (he does!) and you don't know what kind of grade to give him. Write "Pass" on the forms where his grades are supposed to go.

The Giggler

This will be a girl. She's nervous. She's as embarrassed by her affliction as you are exasperated by it. Have her sit in the front row where she can't see so many male students and won't have so much to be nervous about. Have her help you with such mundane chores as sorting papers, alphabetizing cards, and putting out the cut slips for the office girl. If the opportunity should arise, ask her advice about something and follow it.

Genius I

Few school districts reveal scores on scholastic aptitude tests to parents. There are rare cases when they probably should. Tests of this kind measure the student's ability to reason, to distinguish patterns, to discriminate between shades of verbal meaning—in short, his intelligence. The layman, without the figures before him, tends to see evidence of this quality in the wrong things, or to pay too much attention to the right things in the wrong context.

A student we'll call Genius I may be thought by his parents to be brilliant because he learned his arithmetic facts early and learned them extremely well, or because he has a large speaking vocabulary, or perhaps merely because he is the only one in his family who reads at grade level, his brothers and sisters being retarded. The student may not be brilliant at all. His teachers may not even consider him to be bright, just an average kid with a good memory or one who gets his jollies by using big words in all the wrong places. Yet the student conducts himself with the aplomb of an intellectual giant. Why? Because his family has always told him he was an intellectual giant. They told him and told him and told him. The kid has thus developed into a snob with nothing to be a snob about.

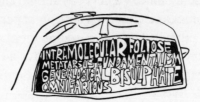

Now, intellectual snobbery is bad enough when the brains and talent are there to justify it, as we shall see pres' ently with Genius II; but when snobbery is rooted in fic' tion, the expected fruit will never mature. Both the student and his parents will harvest disappointment and little else.

The pattern is nearly always the same. In his school work, Genius I and his parents will feel his mediocre grades are reflecting the teacher's ill will. It will never occur to them that his grades are reflecting his own mediocre performance. As he progresses through elementary to secondary school, his lack of ability will become more apparent, and his grades may sink from B's to C's, and perhaps even to D's. The tension between home and school will build.

At home, Genius I is desperately clinging to his treasured status in the bosom of the family and complains bitterly of teachers who won't give him a chance, who deliberately twist things he says, who "have it in for him." When the business can be tolerated no longer the parents march grimly to school, chip on shoulder and blood in eye. Usually, the counselor (lucky man!) will be the one who talks them out of tarring and feathering a teacher or two. He will give them the information they need to bring their expectations of their child into sharper focus, and that will just about be that. But if you have been alert to this problem, you have the power to stop it before it gets that far. Before a month has passed, Genius I's problem will become uncomfortably clear to you.

When he first enters your class, you will assume from his behavior that he is among the brighter students in the group. He will patronize the lesser lights and adopt a stance of leadership quite naturally. His role may be so skillfully played that you may be taken in by it. You simply won't believe your eyes when you grade your first test and his performance turns out to be wretched. If the next two or three weeks confirm that his performance is uniformly as poor as your first sample, invite him in for a conference. Prepare for it by collecting a large group of student papers (twenty minimum), all of which have been checked by you, all of which have the grades prominently displayed on them. Reports, themes, tests, daily drills, and exercises should be included, and should represent a range from A to F in quality. Turn over the corners of the papers so the names can't be seen if you like, but this isn't absolutely necessary. Have three or four of Genius I's papers there, too.

"Algernon," you will open the interview. "Do you understand why it is you are making C's and D's in my classes?"

"No, indeed, I do not, and what's more, I . . ."

"I thought perhaps you didn't. So I got some things together here that might be of interest to you."

Arrange the specimens from A papers down to F papers. Let him look and read and look and read and look some more. He will ask a few questions.

"What's so great about this paper it got a A?"

Tell him.

"My handwriting ten times improve over this'n here and you gimme a C and you give him a B. How come?"

Tell him.

When he seems to have seen enough and is ready to go, say, "Algernon, I'd like very much to invite your parents to come to school to talk about your grades. I'll bet they're disappointed that you're not doing better in your school-work, aren't they?"

"Yeah. They disappointed."

"Would you object if I phoned your mother and asked her to come to school one afternoon next week? And your father, too, if he can get away."

"Well . . . let me consult her when I gits home this after-noon and see what she say."

"All right. And will you let me know tomorrow?"

Either Algernon will decide to handle the matter as best he can by himself—"She says she awful preoccupied pres-ently, can she come sometime later?"—or he will chicken out and let you do it your way—"She say she exaggerated you invite her. What day?"

If she comes, make arrangements for the counselor to be present with you at this interview. It's unwise for a new teacher to handle a parent-teacher conference alone if there is any likelihood of ill feeling. After the necessary points have been covered, you should excuse yourself and let the counselor talk to her alone.

Afterwards, if Algernon is half as bright as he pretends to be, he'll tell his parents "I sorry I not as smart as you all thought I was," and everybody will have a good cry. A new and better day will dawn—for the family, for Algernon's teachers, and, most important of all, for Algernon himself.

There will be other cases where the solution to the prob-lem won't be nearly this simple. Algernon's self-image is at stake. Since birth he has believed he was a Superior Person, and his terror of admitting, especially to himself, that he is just about like everybody else will lead him to resort to every known defense. Over the years, Genius I becomes an expert at cheating. He will learn the advantages of being a slow and methodical worker ("Let me take it home and copy it over" and also correct all the mistakes). He will learn to be sick on test days and will quickly cry foul if the teacher doesn't give him the same test for make-up that was given to the other students two days before.

It's quite possible for the problem to be so deeply-rooted that the student faces severe emotional disturbance if forced to admit his own inadequacies. He literally *must* kid himself if he is to survive at all. To know and accept himself for what he is would require months, perhaps years, of psycho-therapy, treatment the school is in no position to provide. In this case, about all the school can do is suffer along with him until he graduates. And he will, never fear. You won't see how he'll wangle it, but he will.

Genius II

It's unfair to devote an entire book to troublesome adolescents and say nothing whatever about the other kind. For every teen-ager who causes headaches in the school, there will be twenty-five middlegrounders and at least half a dozen at the opposite end of the spectrum who are absolute jewels, without whom it's difficult to see how the school would function at all. They are the school's pacesetters, sparkplugs, and errand-runners. They enjoy sound mental as well as physical health and discipline themselves from a rich fund of common sense. They show up promptly every morning, scrubbed, co-operative, and enthusiastic, with heads chock full of dandy little ideas that work.

Many (not all) of these jewels will score in the upper brackets on the scholastic aptitude tests. Their parents are bright, too, not only about books but about everything, including the way they bring up their offspring. Typically, behavior problems are rare among these bright students, the most serious being an unbecoming tendency toward mouthiness. In college prep groups, classroom buzz becomes classroom roar in the time it takes the papers to be passed to the front of the room. Annoying, but scarcely threatening if kept under control.

Truly bright youngsters seem to come with built-in *noblesse oblige*. It's a hallmark of the ultra-bright student that distinguishes him from the medium-bright one. They shrink, these sharpies, from using their superior minds in ways that hurt others. As a group, they tend to be remarkably free of malice themselves or the suspicion of malice in others— sometimes to the point of gullibility. They will almost never discuss their brains or spend time worrying about what is worthy of their intelligence and what isn't.

The arrogant, overbearing parvenu with an I.Q. of 140 or better is as hard to find as edelweiss in southern Arizona. And that's good, because if you ever have the misfortune to draw one of these in a class, you will come to welcome him every day as you would a bad case of hives. We'll call him Genius II.

The big difference between Genius I and Genius II is that the teacher, *any* teacher, is usually smarter than Genius I, whereas Genius II may match his teachers in intelligence or even beat them. Not only does Genius II know this, he never lets his teachers forget it. He uses his intelligence daily to degrade and bully them into submission.

Genius II is a loner by choice. His tastes are too refined for him to associate with his peers in the honors class; he considers them immature, even though they are often brighter than he is. School rules, he maintains, are for clods and are not to be tolerated by creative, sensitive persons of his caliber. The curriculum itself, and above all, the teachers who present it, are geared to the ordinary and cannot be expected to appeal to the extraordinary (him), even though the school may take particular pride in its college-prep track. He drags his feet on schoolwork because he's saving himself for the brilliant, talented professors who await him at Harvard (or Cal, Yale, Princeton, etc.). He has been saving himself for so long, in fact, and blackmailing his teachers for grades for so long, that he is actually a very poorly educated person! He can't express either concrete ideas or abstractions on paper, much less punctuate them properly or spell the words correctly. He isn't sure if James Russell Lowell was American or British, or if Shakespeare and Chaucer were contemporaries. His notions of mathematical functions and physical laws are hazy at best and totally inaccurate at worst.

When you confront Genius II with the gaps in his educational background, he will tell you he is interested in theoretical work and prefers not to clutter up his mind with the rote-learned trivia of public school education. You may wonder how he plans to get into college at all with no more preparation than he has, but then you will remember his straight A record (What teacher has dared to give him anything else?) and his truly impressive intelligence test scores.

Your imagination will stagger at the picture of this intellectual freak in a freshman class in any college or university in the land. The temptation will be overwhelming to wash your hands of him and let him flunk out of Harvard, where, with stiffer competition, he will automatically shift classifications from Genius II (somebody special) to a point even below Genius I (somebody about average).

Coping with the problem is a thorny assignment. The precautions to be observed with Genius II are identical to those observed with Genius I. The matter of ego strength must be gauged, and a talk with his counselor may be profitable. If you feel up to tangling with him and Mama (there's always Mama, I.Q. about 115), you can undertake to educate him. You may insist that he obey the same rules as the other students, turn in work of the same quality and at the same time as the other students, and be graded by the same criteria as the other students—in short, demand that he put up or shut up.

The paper routine recommended for Genius I won't work with Genius II. Genius I and his parents are willing to admit that there are such things as right and wrong answers and that the ability to write a good essay is important. Genius II and Mama will emerge from such a session unscathed. They will insist that tests and themes measure conformity and little else. They convinced themselves long ago that his dynamic intellect far outshone that of his classmates. What they will challenge is not what grades he deserves, but your right, as a mere public servant, to teach him at all!

Don't start your campaign unless you're prepared to follow through all year. You don't need to be more intelligent than he is. After all, you're only trying to teach him what you know, and at the present time he knows considerably less than you do. You need, however, to be more stubborn than he is, and you also need a thick skin; he'll make a monkey of you every time you turn around. It will be a rough fight. Be sure you keep the principal informed about what you're doing and why. Mama will be phoning him, and phoning him, and phoning him.

Genius III

This student is also rare, perhaps rarer than Genius II. You may teach a lifetime and see him only once or twice, or perhaps not at all. He is included here because in the event he does come, it's so terribly important not to let him down.

He's Holden Caulfield. He's equipped with a special kind of vision that enables him to see through phoniness, which he loathes. He's a Truth Seeker and a Truth Teller, which sometimes gets him in trouble with the authorities. Other than his penchant for telling the truth, he's so quiet and unassuming you may not know he's there at all. You won't discover what a unique and amazing person he is until his written work begins to come in.

He probably won't be able to spell, either, but his choice of subject matter will dumbfound you. He'll write about things most adults don't think about, let alone adolescents. What is good, and why does good sometimes turn out to be bad? Is there anything that's important, and if so what? What are we all doing here, anyway?

He isn't being impertinent or glib. He isn't challenging you, as Genius II might be, enticing you into abstractions that are beyond your depth so he can make you look like a jackass. This student wants answers.

Well, you won't be able to supply them, so don't try. You aren't enough like Genius III that your answers will satisfy him at all. He's going to be brainier than you, more creative than you, and far, far more restless than you. The tremendously important thing you can do for him is to head him in the direction of other brainy, creative people via books. Give him Gibran to read, and de Tocqueville, Camus, Joyce, Mumford, Santayana, Kierkegaard, Freud, Gorky,

Baldwin, and Toynbee. You won't always come up with something he digs, but keep trying.

Get him to talk. How is he reacting to what he's reading? Does he disagree with the ideas of these men? Why? If you don't have the mental or educational equipment to discuss these matters with him, for heaven's sake don't make the hideous mistake of pretending you do. There's no need to, anyway. You'll quickly discover he finds weaknesses in his own arguments more quickly than you would. He needs a listener. He's trying on different ideas to see how they fit. He won't find his answers, ever; but by the time he's forty, he will have settled for educated guesses, the most brilliant of which might very well be his own.

God's Gift to Men / Women

Briefly, these types are overstimulated by the opposite sex. Their physicians will say they have hyperactive glands, their counselors will say they are insecure, and their peers will say they have the hot pants. Regardless of the diagnosis, a seductively twitching, eye-rolling lass seated in the midst of half-a-dozen young bucks can play hob with your lesson plan. Move her into the midst of half a dozen other girls. Use similar therapeutic procedures for the scintillating male who has gathered a giggling harem about him; break it up.

A thornier version of this problem comes about when the student isn't soliciting attention at all, but is simply attractive, devilishly so. No matter where you move a truly lovely teen-age girl in a room half full of teen-age boys, the boys will behave like hyenas. If she is demure and feminine, it makes matters worse, not better. A handsome, slim-hipped boy who dresses and moves well can have the same effect on girls. Bury these handsome children out of sight at the back of the room. Use every stratagem you can think of to keep them there. When it's time for oral reports, schedule theirs last. Don't call on them to recite until just before the bell rings.

Cliff Hanger I

It's part of growing up for boys to place themselves in situations of danger for the express purpose of finding if they're man enough to handle it. Girls can have babies; to prove her femininity, all a girl need do is sit there and Mother Nature takes care of everything. But to prove himself a man, a boy must test muscle and wit to the utmost before he can wholly know who and what he is.

Many parents are shrewd enough to realize this, and their sons go out for school sports with their blessings—or take up such hobbies as cave exploring, scuba diving, flying, sky diving, skiing, or herpatology. Though physical risks in these pursuits may be high, the parents reason it is better for the boy to fight it out with an eight-foot anaconda and risk a mangled arm than to race a buddy on the public highway at 125 mph.

The urge to hang-from-cliffs-without-actually-falling varies in degree from individual to individual. The Cliff Hanger Senior Grade wants to find out how far he can go without killing himself. He is reckless beyond the call of duty and inspires awe in the Cliff Hanger Junior Grade, who merely wants to find out how far he can go before he gets caught stealing Pop's bonded bourbon or before he breaks a leg— or before he gets kicked out of school.

The student we are considering sometimes comes to school and sometimes doesn't. He is a master at forging notes from home. Though he cuts classes when he feels like it, which is often, he is never without an "excuse" on his return. He smokes forbidden cigarettes in the restroom, and later comes to class with a green-stained tongue from the chlorophyll gum he is careful to chew.

He has made a thorough study of the rules, classroom rules of individual teachers as well as those of the school at large, and he knows how to circumvent them. His hard luck tales would wring tears from a golf ball, but his protestations of good will have a phony ring, as though he memorized entire paragraphs from *Boy's Life.* He plays teachers off against counselors or against each other with distortions of the truth—or downright lies.

Over the years, his sins accumulate until he inevitably arrives at a point where he isn't actually "in" school at all; he is there so seldom he has lost track of his schoolwork and his teachers have lost track of what he knows and what he doesn't know. From time to time he is caught; but, by the grace of God and his own skill, he hasn't yet been caught in the final transgression that will expel him. So, he isn't "out" of school, either.

This student's situation may become so interesting it provides a staple item of school gossip, both with the faculty in the lounge and the students in the cafeteria: "Have they expelled Fred yet?" This adventure may go on for a couple of years. Incredibly, the kid may even get his diploma and at last prove to the world he prevailed against formidable forces and triumphed, a man indeed!

What should the new teacher do with this character? As

little as possible. Be assured, his life is already so crowded with welfare workers, juvenile court officers, counselors, divorced parents and step-parents, brothers and sisters, step-brothers and step-sisters, plus, perhaps, a pregnant girl or two waiting in the wings (typically, there will be several cliffs he's hanging from simultaneously) that you will make matters worse, not better, by interfering with his problem or by forcing unnecessary issues. Compute his grades as honestly as you know how and send them in. Note his absences and tardies and send them in. When he's there, smile at him.

Necessary issues, of course, are a different matter. Should he become angry about something in your class and swear at you, you must report the matter to SFF, even if it brings the house of cards crashing to the ground. But it's not likely he'll do this. What he'll do instead is *almost* give you cause to report him.

When you see the first signs that the Cliff Hanger has sweet old you pegged as still another cliff it would be fun to hang from, go to his seat for a little exercise in communications.

"Fred," you might say, "I have talked to the other teachers about you. They don't seem to like you much."

"Yeah."

"And I've talked to the assistant principal about you. He doesn't seem to like you much, either."

"Yeah."

"They all tell me you're about to get kicked out of school. Is that right?"

"Yeah."

"All that's needed to kick you out of school is to be sent to the office just one more time by a teacher. That right?"

"Yeah."

"I see."

Fred is pretty good at communications. He will get your message.

Cliff Hanger II

Judged on the basis of superficial behavior alone, this student belongs with the Malingerer and the Timeserver; sometimes it's easy to confuse them. Motive is the differentiating factor. The Malingerer wants a free ride, and he proposes to use your sympathy for a ticket. The Timeserver *at one time* wanted to participate in school and do well, but has resigned himself to failure and is only waiting till the calendar runs its course to get out sans diploma. Cliff Hanger II wants the diploma, always wanted it, but never at any time saw a reason to expend more effort than absolutely necessary to get it. He hangs in the delicate balance between passing and failing. That's exactly where he wants to be. He can be shifted from one curriculum track to another like a handcar, and he will still find his place *almost* at the bottom of the class.

Cliff Hanger II is lazy, bone lazy. It isn't a matter of blood pressure or neurosis, but of values. Physical ease is the *summum bonum*, and his tribal diety is the three-toed sloth. His achievement in class will be lower than his scholastic aptitude scores would lead you to expect. He may be slightly dull or very bright. Indeed, he might one day win a doctorate, having exercised meticulous care along the way to do only what was absolutely necessary to get it.

Typically, he will make C's and D's. When he finds his grade-point sinking to such depths that his diploma is jeopardized, he will argue with you about the mark you gave him. Whatever his grade, if you computed it correctly and there is no reason to change it beyond his pleas for "another chance," refuse to change it. Do nothing beyond what is absolutely necessary (*sic!*) to give him fair grades. Your obligation ends there.

The Operator

There will be the student who apparently went through the line four times when they were passing out aggressive tendencies. This boy will become a sales executive someday and make more money in one year than you make in five. Everywhere he goes, in any situation, under any conditions whatever, he will take over. He will take over your class if you let him.

If the students all like him and willingly accept his leader-ship in the class, you can use him as a sort of unofficial sergeant-at-arms and things will go fairly smoothly. But you'll more often find the other students don't like him and will resent his high-handed ways. Furthermore, you will lose the respect of these other students if you allow him to get out of line.

There is no easy way out. You will have to call him down and call him down, take him out in the hall to talk to him, and no doubt send him to the office fairly often for some moral support from SFF. You can squelch him for short periods. ("My teaching credential is home in my desk; where's yours?") but two days is about all the peace this kind of thing will buy you. Sorry.

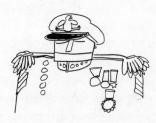

The Transient

In a big high school, at any given time of the morning or afternoon, you will find perhaps three per cent of the student body not in class at all, but walking up and down the halls. Whether it's Monday or Thursday, October or May, it will almost always be the same three per cent. They will be engaged in a variety of pursuits. This one has his teacher's permission to get notebook paper from his locker. That one is on his way to the restroom or (smelling strongly of ciga-rette smoke) has been to the restroom and is on his way back to class. A third, absent yesterday, has "lost" his permit to class and is on his way to the office to get a duplicate. A fourth student "has a headache" and has been excused to go to the nurse. A fifth is "going to the office to see his coun-selor," secure in the knowledge his counselor is away from the school at a meeting. A sixth is cutting class because he hasn't written the report that's due today. A seventh has been summoned to the attendance office to account for the class he cut two days ago. On and on it goes.

With the exception of a few students who will be out of class on legitimate business, such as getting a book from the library or gathering information for the school paper, all of these students will be Transients, young people who have devoted years of thoughtful study and practice to the fine art of getting out of class.

Why do they want to get out of class? Because, as it is traditionally conducted, education is less a process of developing the physical, intellectual, and aesthetic talents of the young than it is a twelve-year poker game in which the intellectually able consistently hold the high cards and win and the not-so-intellectually able consistently hold the low cards and lose. For the winners, the arrangement is just ginger-peachy, but the losers don't like it especially.* They get out of class if they can.

A teacher who deals successfully with Transients must keep them in class and make class so satisfying that they no longer want out.

The first requirement is simple and demands only the stamina to say: "No, you can't be excused to go to the rest-room; wait until the end of the period." "Start on your report now, so you'll have it ready when it's due next week." "Leave word in the office that you want to see your counselor and he'll send for you when he can see you."

The second requirement is harder, because it involves more than superficial things like a pretty room and movies once a week. It has to do with what you really think and feel about education. If you sincerely feel that education is a kind of intellectual rubber-stamping process whose sole justification is that it enables students to get into college and to get a job, do both your Transients and yourself a favor and set them free to wander at will. If, on the other hand, you are convinced that the urge to satisfy one's need for in-

---

* Many public school educators don't like it especially, either, and are forever inventing stratagems to keep the losers from giving up altogether. "Tracking" is one of these stratagems. "Tracking" means that instead of having all the losers concentrated among the ranks of the less able students, they are spread about more democratically throughout the entire student body. With tracking, you can have college prep losers and average losers as well as slow-learner losers. But not really; because the college prep losers can be transferred to the average track if things get too bad, and the average student can be transferred to the slow-learner track. Where can the loser in the slow-learner track go? Same place he could go before anybody thought of tracking—*out*. Conservative types like to point out that this is the way life is, and the sooner young people find it out, the better. But they're wrong. Only a zombie remains in a situation where he fails year after year after year. Even if the student drops out, marries, has seven children, and spends the rest of his life on welfare, he won't be subjected to the corrosive punishment of daily failure he encountered in school.

tellectual stimulation and achievement is more basic than the urge to satisfy physical hunger (a wealth of research proves it is) and that reasons for satisfying one are equally valid for satisfying the other (you don't eat to get into college or to get a job, you do so because your body requires food and you're hungry), then you are equipped with the necessary frame of reference to find out what it is your students want to learn. You are prepared to furnish them with the materials they need to scratch where it itches. The trouble with education is that it does too much scratching where it doesn't itch, and it rubs people raw.

If your Transients can get the information they want from magazines and newspapers, forget the textbook. If they can get it from each other, that's even better—as long as you make sure it's information, not ignorance, that they're sharing.

One more comment before we leave our student stereotypes. Never resent the students who force you to do your best teaching. They'll make a pro out of you. Easy students never taught a teacher anything.

five

Control in the School at Large

Teachers' extra-classroom assignments vary tremendously from school to school. The modern trend, heaven be praised, is to relieve them of the more arduous ones on the eminently sensible theory that if you hire a person to teach, he'll do more of it and do it better if you see that he has the time and strength left to teach. Few schools today, for example, require the teacher to carry in wood and coal and keep the classroom stove going as our predecessors routinely did a century ago.

Typically, a teacher's assignments nowadays might include: selling tickets for and chaperoning sports events and dances; duty in the attendance office; hall, cafeteria, restroom, and bus supervision; sponsorship of clubs; and membership on P.T.A. committees. In all but the last, the teacher bears no responsibility to teach anything and retains only the responsibility for handling discipline. In fact, that's the reason he's there.

Chaperoning and Selling Tickets

Chaperoning sports events and dances can be more fun than a chore. Problems rarely arise; you may attend these affairs for a couple of years and never hear an angry word. Besides that, seeing your students at play is a surprising and delightful experience. The wildest dance on the floor may be executed by the mousy little girl in your third period class. And who turns out to be the best tackle on the second team? The Timeserver you've been worrying about for two weeks!

When you attend such school events, dress appropriately. Your principal expects you to; but more than that, your students expect you to. Although you won't be aware of it, many pairs of eyes will be taking your measure.

"There's my physics teacher over there. See him?"

"The clod in the horse blanket?"

"Naw, you jerk, not him. The guy in the blue suit."

"Oh. *Him.* Looks okay."

For sports affairs, the sort of thing you wear to school is good. Naturally, a tie is required of men, and a dress (not slacks) and nylon stockings for women. This same type of clothing is appropriate for informal "student hops" or "mixers." It is not appropriate, however, for a prom or other formal party. You will *never* be forgiven if you chaperone a formal dance or banquet in a sport shirt, or in flats and a cotton print. This will be a party that has been planned for and looked forward to all year. The girls will have agonized for weeks deciding whether to buy the white taffeta or the blue brocade formal. The boys will have spent sweaty hours earning money for corsages and for a post-dance treat. Intricate arrangements will have been made concerning the music, the ballroom decorations, the Grand March, and the selection of the master of ceremonies. For a chaperone to treat all this as just one more throwaway evening is a cruel affront.

It is an equally bad mistake for women teachers to move too far in the opposite direction. Don't try to match the girls' party finery; try to make a fitting background for them. Something subdued and dark is about right. Heels are mandatory for women. Men should definitely wear suits and ties.

Students will ask you to dance. The better part of valor is to decline with a smile and a plausible excuse. ("My wife doesn't like me to dance with beautiful girls.") These affairs are for the students, not the faculty. There is something unseemly about a faculty member who cavorts and gambols with his charges. The price he pays in damaged prestige is too high for the fun he has.

Look around from time to time, although it may be hard to remember to do so if it's a good game you're supervising. Investigate students who have gathered in a knot behind the bleachers to watch something. Find out what the something is they're watching. Break it up if it shouldn't be going on.

Be alert for loud arguments. They grow into fights and then into full-scale rumbles, and it can happen while you take the time to summon a policeman. Don't wait that long. Get to it immediately while it's still at the argument stage. Collect ID cards from the students involved. Straighten it out on the spot, if you can. If not, take the students with you to find the vice-principal.

Most schools keep a uniformed policeman on duty just in case. He is seldom needed, primarily because he's *there*.

Although women teachers are usually excused from the tougher assignments at these gatherings, one wonders if they should be. An angry woman strikes as much awe in students as an angry man, and sometimes more.

Watch out for booze, visitors, and weapons, in that order. Intoxicants will most often be brought on the premises by girls, not boys; they have more places to hide a bottle. Once inside, your nose will tell you which students are drinking.*

Having a big dance at a school is like turning on a light: it attracts bugs from miles around. Toughs from other schools, and former students from your own school who have been expelled or who have dropped out, take this opportunity to stir up a little excitement. Since they aren't bona fide students, there is virtually no way to control them once admitted. Usually, school policy forbids admitting them at all. They will hang around the building or the parking lot if they aren't chased away, which is why supervision is necessary over the entire area, not just the room where the dance is being held.

If only enrolled students are admitted, there will be no problem with weapons. The students will tend to abide by the same rules that govern them when classes are going on during the day, and penalties for carrying weapons are severe.

---

* Of course you will be able to detect the odor because you won't have been drinking yourself. The teacher who drinks before coming to a school affair or after he gets there is so foolish as to defy comment.

If drinks are dispensed via machine in bottles, the empty bottles should be returned to their cases promptly and not left at random over the premises. A better plan is to have a refreshment stand as close to the dance area as possible to provide drinks in paper cups. You can't split anybody's head open with a paper cup.

Students should not be allowed to leave the dance area with drinks. A common practice is to sweeten them up from the incriminating bottle left in the car outside or in the restroom.

The only thing to do about a full-scale rumble is to get as much help as possible and then wade into the middle of the fracas and pull kids apart. Keep yelling something that sounds official, like "Break it up, break it up," so they'll know you're a teacher. Look for the kids with the weapons and get them first. The ones who started it will probably be the hardest of all to stop. Get them to the office or to a room away from the rest of the mob where everybody can cool off and talk sense. Get the vice-principal and let him handle it. Go back out and help disperse the crowd.

Boys' fights are never as spontaneous as they appear to be on the surface. They represent an accumulation of less-than-fight-sized resentments that finally build up intolerable pressure. If the pressure is strong enough, a trivial remark can trigger a fight. Typically, one boy will bully and taunt another over a long period of time. At length, the bully pushes his luck too far and the underdog fights back. Rivalries between schools can build in this way and erupt in fights.

When boys fight they pound each other and break a few bones, if possible. Girls' fights are bloodier and messier. They claw, tear, gouge, and rip. There might be a whole army of boys involved in a fight, but there will never be more than two girls.

Boys get into fights on their own, but for girls there's always a "promoter."

"Julia said you were two-faced."

"Julia's more two-faced than I ever thought about being."

"Kathy said you were the most two-faced b – – – – that ever walked."

"You tell Kathy for me her mother should have flushed her down the john before she was a week old."

"Julia said she'd like to flush you down the john."

"She did, did she? I'd like to see her try it, that dirty no-good #@$%!!!"

"Kathy's going to beat you up."

"Just tell me when and where and we'll see about that."

"This afternoon after school. There's a good place in the alley behind the grocery store."

The promoter will hustle up a crowd and may or may not stop short of selling tickets. SFF will be looking for the promoter, and so should you if it falls your job to round everybody up.

Selling tickets at the game or dance, however, is pretty tame for the teacher. The worst hazards are frostbite, if the ticket booth is drafty, and that limp feeling when you realize you gave a customer ten dollars' worth of change for his five. Things are slow after the game starts. Bring a magazine.

Suppose you have been assigned duty at an evening activity and a wheel drops off your car and you simply can't make it. Be sure to let someone in authority know, just as you would if you couldn't take your classes during the day. If your assignment turns out to be terribly inconvenient, offer to exchange assignments with another teacher. It isn't unheard-of for enterprising young (and less well-paid) teachers to do a flourishing business taking unwanted duty assignments for a fee.

Attendance Office Duty

The attendance office keeps up with who's at school, who's not, and why not. A teacher on duty in the attendance office may check excuses from home for students returning after an absence, issue admit-to-class slips, or telephone parents to inquire after students currently absent. Some of the replies will jar you a bit.

"Mrs. Anderson, I'm phoning from the attendance office at school to find out why Ron is absent today."

"His leg's in Oregon."

"How's that again?"

"He wears a false leg. A hinge came loose and we sent it to Oregon to be fixed. He can't walk until it gets back."

A million laughs.

Hall, Cafeteria, and Bus Duty

Hall duty simply means walking a beat. It's a good time for making grocery lists or organizing next week's lesson plans. You may be asked to patrol the hall immediately outside your classroom door while students are passing from one class to another. Whether this is required or not, it's good psychology to greet your students at the door. The gesture evokes the same overtones as a host with his guests. "You are expected and welcome," it says, and your students will sit up a bit straighter because you gave them that feeling.

Like hall duty, nothing much is likely to happen when your turn comes to supervise the cafeteria during lunch period. You may need to remind a few negligent youngsters to do whatever it is they're supposed to do with their trays. If a student makes a mess, make him clean it up. There's not a chance in fifty an argument will start. But if it does, break it up *immediately*. A cafeteria is the messiest place imaginable for a rumble.

When you're on bus duty, all you do is watch the busses drive up, load, and drive off. Holler a little if the students seem inclined to shove.

Restroom Duty

Women teachers have a rougher time of it than men when it comes to restroom duty. Girls throw used paper towels on the floor, foul the basins with hair combings, and write filthy poems on the walls.

If you catch a student contributing to the pigsty effect, make her clean it up, of course. Report the filthy poem to the vice-principal, who will have the custodian remove it as soon as possible before it inspires still another Emily Dickinson to add a couplet or two.

Your school will probably be careful about cleaning off all markings on walls, etc., daily. This is partly because one good mark encourages another if you don't get rid of the first one. But it is also because if you know the restroom was clean at the beginning of the day it's easier to find the culprit if it is *not* clean at, say, 9 A.M. You narrow the field down to the people who were there during an hour and a half, instead of suspecting the people who were there over a two-day period.

Smoking is the big problem in the restrooms. Both state laws and school policy throw the book at students caught with cigarettes or smoking on the school premises. In middle- and upper-class neighborhoods, it isn't hard to enforce these rules; but in areas where the median family income is $3,000 a year or less, you'd expel half the student body if you did. All you can do is punish the glaring offenses and nit-pick away at the others in a battle no one will ever win.

When you enter a restroom and witness two or three students actually holding cigarettes; collar them immediately and take them to the office. If there's smoke but no visible cigarettes, station yourself by the door and have a look in all the girls' purses or all the boys pockets as they leave.

If you are assigned total supervisory responsibility for one restroom—say, across the hall from your classroom—don't be so regular about it that the smokers can set their watches by you. One day check at 9:15, 1:30, and 3, next day, at 8:30, 9:00, and 2. Report all incidents of smoking and vandalism to the vice-principal.

Club Sponsorship

Running a student activity can be a business in itself. The yearbook organization may maintain an office, hire clerical help, and collect and disburse thousands of dollars a year. Sponsorship of clubs and activities is nearly always on a volunteer basis; the more experienced teachers are favored for the bigger assignments, which sometimes yield a modest stipend. This is a blessing in disguise for the first-year teacher, who will have more corn than he can hoe, anyway.

Once he has his classes under control, the new teacher might find it valuable to ally himself with an older, experienced teacher-sponsor in the role of assistant—a painless way to learn the student activity ropes. He may, of course, be assigned a small club the first year. This is not such a painless way to learn the ropes. But if he finds out what to do about the money and does it, and obtains extra supervisory help with parties, cookouts, and the like, he should get along all right. He would do well to remember that in a club, you let down—but only about halfway.

Sponsoring a student organization means that sooner or later you must ask other teachers to excuse your members from class to do something about the club. Protocol must be observed in such matters. First of all, get your principal's permission for the students to be out of class. Secondly, about ten days before the trip, type up a ditto master that runs something like this:

Dear_____,

On Thursday, October 26, from 1 P.M. to 4 P.M., the Chess Club members would like to attend the state chess tournament being held in our city. Club members understand that they may go only with the permission of their teachers and with the understanding they are to make up work missed in classes that day.

Our club roster is as follows:

(List of members)

If you are willing to excuse these students from your classes that afternoon, will you please initial this letter and return it to the student presenting it?

Cordially yours,
(Your name)
Chess Club sponsor

Fill in the appropriate teacher's name and assign one student per teacher to deliver the forms one day and pick them up the next. If there seems to be an objection anywhere, go around to see the teacher personally and answer any question he has. You will nearly always be able to work through any difficulties together. Be sure to thank the teacher for his co-operation.

The new teacher, in his turn, will be on the receiving end of requests from other club sponsors. He should co-operate, if possible, but he isn't expected to co-operate to the point of completely rejuggling his lesson plans. If many students are involved and it means a real inconvenience for him, he should go to the sponsor as soon as possible and see what can be worked out. Maybe the sponsor can change his date.

The P.T.A.

One day your principal will call you into his office and ask you if you will serve on the P.T.A. refreshment or program committees. Since he heads up the "T" part of the P.T.A., he must furnish personnel to help make the things go.

Don't be surprised if you discover your committee work is more enjoyable than the monthly meetings you will be helping to put on. Oddly enough, the most successful junior and senior high school P.T.A.'s you hear of around the country seem to be the ones with the fewest meetings—say, once a year.

The once-a-year pattern hasn't swept the nation like wildfire. ("It takes fifty years for an idea, etc.") Typically, a handful of souls will clip-clop their way through the school's deserted evening corridors to hear a nice lady report there is $26.15 in the treasury, after which a panel of adolescents will explain how the school's student government works. Coffee or punch will be served in the home economics room, and everybody will say what a shame there wasn't a better turnout to hear the nice program. Afterwards, they'll drive home swearing on a stack of old roadmaps never to come to one of these meetings again.

Some principals, as a pump-priming device, let it be known that teachers are expected to be at the P.T.A. meeting. This is a good way to get out a crowd of teachers, but it makes for soggy morale in the long run. It puts the outnumbered parents on the defensive, and soon you've got a monthly teacher's meeting.

The chances of seeing the parents of your students at the average P.T.A. meeting are about one in fifty. However, there will be a big, full-dress Parent's Night sometime in the fall, which may or may not be sponsored by the P.T.A. The classrooms will be open, with teachers inside and available for parent-teacher conferences. These are often well attended—never by the parents you need most to see, of course—but you may put in a busy evening chatting with mamas and papas. Be a good host. Meet as many people at the door as you can. Invite them in and ask them to sit down. You will have written your name on the chalkboard, but introduce yourself anyway. "How do you do? I'm Mr. Lansdale. It's so good of you to come. I'll be with you in just a minute."

Most parents will simply introduce themselves as "Ted Smith's parents." After a few pleasantries, they will ask if Ted is doing all right, whereupon you will consult your gradebook, if necessary, and reassure them that he is. Kids with parents interested enough to come to meet their teachers usually are.

Rarely, you will have parents whose children are in difficulties. Get the student's papers, your gradebook, or whatever you need from your desk and sit down with these people somewhere else in the room besides your desk. If you seat yourself behind your desk, it implies that somehow the parents are students, too, and you are demanding things of them. You want to establish rapport, but you won't do it that way.

Of all the allies you can enlist in helping you to handle a student in your classroom, none will be more valuable than that student's parents. Parents can see that the homework gets done, that the student gets to school on time, and that he gets enough sleep so he doesn't doze off in class. Most important of all for the purposes of this book, ties of friendship and support at home can virtually eliminate that student's misbehavior in your classroom.

Extra effort spent talking to parents, explaining, listening —in making your room, your students' records, and your teaching materials reflect your competence as a teacher—is bread cast on the waters that keeps returning again and again.

Show the parents first of all that you respect their son or daughter as a fellow human being; show them you know his strengths and weaknesses and know what to do about them —in short, that you know your business. Enlist their support as partners in a joint enterprise, helping their son or daughter to achieve as much as possible in school.

It's a good idea to rub elbows with people in the community where you teach. Whether you live there or not, you can trade there, get to know the gas station people, the barber, and the druggist. Let them know you are a booster, that their tax dollars are staying in the community.

You can go to church in your school community, and this is an even better way to get to know the adults there. As sure as you're born, though, you'll be asked to teach a Sunday school class of students you've taught all week. Resist this. Teaching is what you do for a living, and Sunday should be a day of rest for you, too.

Six

In Loco Parentis

An old pro with twenty-five years of teaching experience once said: "If both the mother and the father are strict, the kid's all right; if both the mother and the father are lenient, the kid's all right. But when one parent is strict and the other parent is lenient, watch out!"

One strict and one lenient parent need not produce a neurotic child as long as both parents agree between themselves on compromises and stick to them. Loyalty of the parents to each other is the key factor. When there is no such loyalty, then "watch out," indeed.

To guarantee good school-wide discipline, the one factor that probably outweighs all others is the willingness of teachers and administrators to support one another. Failure to do this can seriously undermine the morale of both faculty and students.

Students may find themselves in threatening situations where a permissive teacher or counselor whom they scarcely know offers to plot with them against a strict teacher, or where permissive teachers plot with them against a strict principal.

"Sure, I come over here to the sandwich shop every day for lunch. The place is jammed with students even though it's supposed to be off limits. The kids know I won't squeal of them, don't you kids? That story about their selling dope over here is silly."

The student who sees the teacher at the sandwich shop will ask two kinds of questions: (1) "If the principal of the school is such a jerk he can't get his teachers to do what he says, why should I do what he says?" or (2) "That teacher is just as liable to get into trouble as I am. When he does, will he think one of us squealed on him? What will he do then? Is he really what he says he is, the student's pal, or is he some kind of spy? Who's side is he on, anyway?"

"If Mr. A. must have his precious report tomorrow, get your sister to write it for you and come on to the club meeting."

The student asks: (1) "If it's all right to cheat on a report for Mr. A., then it must be okay to cheat every place else. Why should I knock myself out?" or (2) "But if Mr. A. finds out my sister wrote the report, who'll get the blame for it? Suppose I tell Mr. B I want to go home and write the report and not go to the club meeting, will he get sore and see that I don't go on the club trip next week?"

Multiply incidents like this by a dozen or so every day, sprinkled liberally over the school from the P.E. department to the counselors' offices, and you will have an institution peopled with insolent, rebellious teen-age cynics as sure as God made little apples. "Watch out!"

Presenting a united front to students does not imply that all teachers in the school must be of one mind at all times on all issues. Even if it were possible to achieve such agreement, would it be desirable? Diversity of opinion doesn't reflect weakness; it reflects strength.

To re-evaluate presently-agreed-upon policies in the proper place and at the proper time is necessary for the development and modification processes that should take place in any healthy institution. But to encourage students to practice insubordination with implied (but not guaranteed!) promises of immunity is a coward's way of doing business. If the teacher-sponsor of the club isn't man enough to confront Mr. A. himself to ask for extra time for the student to write the report, he has no shred of justification for putting the student on the spot by ordering him to cheat.

Too many people are drawn to teaching not because they want to teach, but because they want to be loved. A dangerous motive. When the teacher's hunger for the approbation of his students outweighs his concern for their best interests, he tends to cast himself in the unbecoming role, not of a parent, but of an irresponsible older brother. And then, "watch out!"

There are many ways the new teacher can avoid falling into this trap. First, he can firmly align himself with other teachers and members of the school staff to be sure he is serving properly *in loco parentium* as well as *in loco parentis*.

Second, the new teacher should realize that he has many mistakes to make before he earns the right to speak with authority about which school rules are proper and which are not. He would be wise to resist the temptation to pass judgment on the competence of his fellow teachers at a time when his own competence is at the lowest point it will ever be.

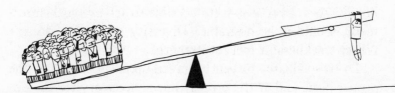

Third, the new teacher should take tale-bearing students with a grain of salt. The adolescent ego is fragile, often requiring reinforcement that is more apt to be fancy than plain. There may be some truth to the story he tells you about the chalk-throwing incident in Mr. A's room, but there may also be some truth that's *left out* of what he tells you. If for some reason you need to get the straight story of the incident, ask for Mr. A's version. The best policy is to discourage this kind of gossiping at all, either with students or with teachers.

Occasionally, two teachers will find themselves competing for a student's time. Perhaps you have told a student he must stay after school and bring his lab notebook up to date. He says he can't because Mr. B told him to stay after school for *him* to do his math assignment. Don't waste everyone's time sending this student back and forth with messages. Go see the teacher yourself with the student in tow. Make your arrangements with Mr. B so that everyone understands what the student is to do and when.

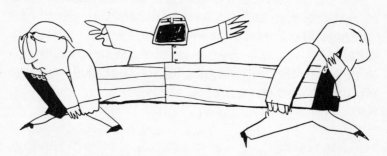

Making derogatory statements to your classes about assemblies, the athletic program, the school in general, is a pernicious sort of nitpicking that boomerangs by contributing to low school morale and increased control problems.

To announce "This class did 20% better than Mr. C's class on the biology test" delivers a gratuitous slap at Mr. C and effectively diminishes his prestige with his students,

each and every one of whom you may be quite sure will hear
the jolly news. It is better to say "This class did quite well
on the biology test," which serves the same purpose with
less malice.

If crystal balls could be checked from the A-V department, you would discover that twenty-five years from now
there will be some present members of the college-prep track
who will have descended to Skid Row and some present
members of the slow-learner track who will be making five-
figure salaries. Tracks should be taken seriously as a teaching
convenience; that's all. As prognosticators of future student
success, they are pretty poor. As indicators of the intrinsic
worth of either students or teachers assigned to them, they
are hopeless.

Before you make snide remarks to your students about the
bottom track, bear in mind that some of the college-prep
history students you're talking to may be enrolled in basic
mathematics courses.

Avoid putting on airs if you are assigned a gifted class.
You might look silly. Some districts start all beginners there
because a novice teacher can do less damage to the gifted
than any other group. The gifted will learn in spite of his
mistakes.

"We're late to class because Mr. D made us do twenty-
five push-ups for being noisy."

Privately, you may react to this information in a number
of different ways, one of which might be to resolve to see
Mr. D before the day is over to find out what really happened. Regardless of your feeling about it, however, you
would be well-advised to comment, "Probably did you good.
Now take your seats and let's get started or I may have you
do twenty-five more."

"My counselor wouldn't even answer my question. He
just walked off and left me standing there. A counselor's
not supposed to act like that. Can't I report him?"

"Maybe he walked off because he was going someplace to report you."

"My math teacher is an old crab and he doesn't even try to understand his students. Can I transfer to your class?"

"I've got news. I'm just as crabby as the math teacher you've got now, and I don't understand you either. You're better off where you are."

The new teacher should make every attempt to get to know the counselors, particularly those of his more trouble-some students. It's tragic that so few teachers take time to do this. The counselor seldom hears anything but the student's version—the *aggrieved* student's version—of what goes on in the classroom. Since the counselor is seldom in the classroom himself, he tends to forget his own years of teaching and the pressures that hour-to-hour, day-to-day teaching engender. He comes to expect teachers, who must handle the student as one in a group of twenty-five, and the administrator, who must handle him as one in fifteen hundred, to exercise the same understanding tolerance he himself is able to command when talking to the student alone in the privacy of his office. With a steady diet of student confidences and virtually no teacher confidences at all, he comes to see all his students a good bit whiter than they really are, and both teachers and administrators as a good bit blacker than they really are.

The counselor's role, under the best of circumstances, is not a happy one. His philosophy and training doom him to march in one direction, yet he must somehow manage to remain on speaking terms with the rest of the school caravan, which is equally doomed by its sheer bulk to march in the opposite direction. He rests squarely on the horns of the individual-versus-society dilemma, which hasn't been resolved in the last ten thousand years and isn't likely to be resolved in the next ten thousand. In fact, as our secondary schools unify and expand, the conflict will grow worse, not better. The bigger the school, the more rules are required, the greater the necessity for the student to conform.

It is the teacher and the counselor, therefore, who are most likely to be dissident school "parents" of the student. To avoid conflicts that will work against the best interests of the student, they must agree on compromises and deal with the student as an adult team.

Looking Ahead

Fifty-one per cent of first-year teachers do not expect to remain in the classroom for as long as five years. The many researchers who have investigated the problem of teacher dropout have looked for answers in the marriage factor among women, low salaries, and such other possibilities as pupil load. Search the literature as you may, you will find no investigation to discover if it could be simply because teaching is devilish hard work!

The enormous physical demands, plus the do-it-immediately-if-not-before emotional pressure, plus the social strain of adjusting to hundreds of quasi-strangers, plus the noise— all these elements take their toll. Outsiders are wont to complain that teachers are sluggish and ultra-conservative; they aren't sluggish and ultra-conservative, they're tired!

The new teacher will begin to realize what he's gotten himself into around Thanksgiving of his first year. His training will have prepared him to cope with his responsibilities. But whether or not his morale and his physical stamina will support maximum use of that training is another question.

What does all this have to do with control? Everything. When a teacher begins to tire, to suffer from months and years of accumulated fatigue, the first place it shows is in his discipline. He has more trouble finding time for conferences with the counselor about problem students. He becomes negligent about following up on petty offenses. He takes refuge in haranguing students rather than actually coming to grips with problems in constructive ways. His classes tend to get out of hand and he thinks, "They're a little loud today." As the months pass, and his students become successively "a little louder," he is able to teach them "a little less." One erosion feeds the other.

The more progressive schools, in their concern to protect teaching efficiency over ten to forty-year periods, make administrative provision for avoiding "teacher erosion." It is not uncommon nowadays to hear of schools that grant sabbaticals, that actively encourage "teacher exchanges," that grant leaves of absence for teachers to work at jobs away from the district, or that maintain a policy of moving teachers from assignment to assignment within the school district.

Whether he becomes conscious of the problem at the end of two months, two years, or twenty years of teaching, however, there is much the teacher himself can do to avoid battle fatigue. (That's all it is, really.)

He needs a hobby, for one thing. Listening to phonograph records or (if the teacher is a lady) hooking rugs won't do; the mind is still free to brood about school problems. The activity must be absorbing, must call for physical and mental activity, not passivity. Bowling, gourmet cooking with a congenial group, reading, carpentry, painting, and choral singing are all good.

Keep in training. Get enough sleep; eat a balanced diet; get the proper exercise. The demands of teaching are rigorous even for a person in good health. A sick man will crumple out of shape in no time at all.

Try to arrange matters so you don't have to take courses at night while school is going on, ever. This is especially true during your first year. This is entirely too big a dose of new educational experiences to absorb at one time. You won't learn much, either from your professor or from your new students.

You will probably need to pick up courses in summer school (doesn't everybody?). Try to schedule the ones you need so you won't go all summer and return to school in the fall as exhausted as when you left at the beginning of summer. Make the time that you spend on the college campus with real honest-to-goodness adults count. You'll pick up as many new ideas from the other students in your classes as you will from the professor. Have coffee with them; study with them. The best ploy of all is to find a principal in the class who's fifty miles or more from home. (Not a local product; he'll be afraid you might quote him.) Buy him a couple of beers and get him to talk shop. You'll *really* learn about education.

Take a course in something unrelated to your field but that you've always wanted to know more about—music appreciation, ceramics, Egyptology, investments, Elizabethan poets, swimming, archaeology, etc.

Get away from home. Load up the family and take a float trip down a river, camp out in the mountains, rent an inexpensive cabin on the lake, visit your brother in Florida, teach summer school in another city (*not* your own district!).

Allow yourself a week to get ready for school in the fall when you go back. Go through your files; throw away things you know you won't use again. Develop teaching ideas and new lesson plans; revise your old tests; work out

that new bulletin board display. Write companies for cata-
logs or examination copies of books; write to that expert in
your field or a former professor for a point of information
you aren't sure about. Set up your calendar for the year.
Approximately when will you need to order this? When will
you check out that? When will you invite the guest
speakers?

Do you like your room arrangement the way it is? Is your
desk farther from the door than you'd like it to be? Do the
students get afternoon sun in their eyes? Are you tired of
the pictures? Change things around.

Most important, try to see it all as a whole. "What am I
doing and why?" Teaching isn't like running a grocery store
or filling teeth or selling insurance. Maybe it's more like
farming than anything else. Every year there's a new crop.
"Success" means the crop grew and flourished and "failure"
means it didn't. The growing season is grueling, backbreak-
ing work. Teachers and farmers don't rest much over week-
ends, as others do, but once a year, during the off-season.

There are good years and bad years. There are years when
the seed is right, the soil perfect, the rains on time, and the
farmer can do no wrong. Other years everything he does is
wrong. Both farmers and teachers learn to accept these
cycles, even to exploit them.

One perseveres. Last year's mistakes inspire this year's
experiments, which in turn yield next year's wisdom. So, one
grows with the growing, finds renewal in the renewed.
Perhaps that's why teachers and farmers live longer than
other people do. It's a good life, after all.

index

121